DARE TO BE YOU,

authorolearywrites

DARE TO BE YOU,

authorolearywrites

A collection of short stories and essays that
will enlighten,inform, and delight your heart, and
hopefully, make "YOU" feel good about being "YOU"!
ISN'T IT TIME YOU FELT GOOD? SHALL WE BEGIN?

Daniel G. O'Leary

authorHOUSE®

AuthorHouse™ LLC
1663 Liberty Drive
Bloomington, IN 47403
www.authorhouse.com
Phone: 1-800-839-8640

Published by AuthorHouse   11/22/2013

ISBN: 978-1-4918-3849-5 (sc)
ISBN: 978-1-4918-3850-1 (e)

Library of Congress Control Number: 2013921757

Disclaimer; All works are original pieces written and published by the author on his blog, authorolearywrites.blogspot.com, on the dates indicated.

Dedications

This book is dedicated to my wife Diane, and our family;
Joe, Michael, Anna, Theresa, Michelle, and Danny.

Without them, their love, and our FAITH and BELIEF
in GOD above, never would it have been possible.

My wife's tireless efforts to balance family, work, caring
for her Mother while assisting others in need, was truly an
inspiration to me! She is my Superwoman, and I thank GOD
every day for having blessed me with her in my life!

CONTENTS

This book is "a collection of short stories and essays that will enlighten, inform, and delight your heart, and hopefully, make "YOU" feel good about "YOU".

A special thanks to Dana Suchow Platin for suggesting I write this book to my wonderful wife Diane. Together, you inspired me to begin. Thank-you both!

Daniel G. O'Leary Destined to Write

I have been writing since I was 10 years old and absolutely love it! Writing is my voice, it has afforded me the opportunity to be heard by family, friends, and the World Community.

My Father, a published writer himself, told me when I was 10, "to put my words in writing and I would always be heard". I took his advice, and he was right!

Often people think and feel insignificant. "Nothing" could be further from the truth! Every single one of us is "significant", does have a purpose, and "will" make a difference. As history has shown, some people make a bigger difference than others. But it has also shown, that a simple act of kindness or hatred by any person, can have a monumental, life altering affect on other people around them. That influence alone, makes any and all of us significant!

My life experiences eventually caused me to look within my heart in search of what I was most passionate about. For me, it was the desire to be a positive influence on others through my writing. I want my words to help, not hurt, to encourage, not discourage, to stimulate creativity and action, not to shatter dreams and prevent progress!

By my word written well, shall I "not" go to hell, for a positive influence they will tell!

Have a great day!

1. CHOICES

Often as we go about our busy days and nights, cramming and rushing to accomplish tasks, priorities, doing and saying that which we believe to be must be done in ever so timely a fashion, it is so easy to miss or simply be blind to one very simple truth; LIFE GOES ON, WITH US OR WITHOUT US, Life of FAMILY, of FRIENDS, of PEOPLE like YOU and me!

Days turn into weeks, weeks into months, months into years, years into decades, and before WE know it, WE hear words of condolence for the passing of another!

So very significant are WE to so many, for WE all touch the lives of thousands, especially those that WE allow to be FRIENDS on Social networking sites such as Face book (to include OUR FAMILY close and far). WE didn't get FRIENDED by ourselves, the other person accepted their request. Either way, as never before can FAMILY and FRIENDS near and far share and celebrate LIFE, laugh, joke, dream, be triumphant, be angry, be sad, be thoughtful, be an ass, be themselves!

To share a photo of a newborn child, of an engagement, of graduation, of beauty, of grace, of so much LIFE that is being lived!!!!

Opportunity abounds to discover that which is seen and experienced by another, and to pass it on to share with others as well. Opportunity to warm another's heart, put a smile upon their face, inspire them to be that which they dare to be. Opportunity to reach out in word, in song, in video to those YOU love and tell them just that; YOU LOVE THEM, and if all the time they have is just a quick hello or "gotta run", it's good enough because it's them that said it or wrote it!

A timely prayer, an instinctive warning, the sharing of a lesson learned, a FAITH found, a PAUSE to capture the wealth of LOVE found, and the excitement to then share it singing praise all the while for having been so well blessed!

Choices do WE all have, choices do WE all make, LIFE will go on with US or without US. WE have chosen (at some point), to be connected, rejoice and experience that which LIFE has to offer!

DARE TO BE YOU, and I'LL DARE TO BE ME, and what a difference will WE all make! Psst—Smile, OUR World's watching!

Shall WE begin?

2. FUNDAMENTAL PRINCIPAL OF SUCCESS; "LIVING WITHIN YOUR MEANS"

The road to financial success is based upon one fundamental principal that is timeless; "Live within your means". You, as an individual, as a family, a community, a town, a State, a Nation, must live within your means to be successful financially.

In OUR Nation, Freedom allows US the opportunity to find that which WE as individuals are passionate about, to dream of that which is possible, to choose to pursue our dream, to continue in our pursuit of fulfilling that dream, but there is a cost; sacrifices are made in the pursuit.

You evaluate where you are, what you have, what you need, what you will need to start your pursuit. You make a plan, understanding that adjustments will still need to be made along the way, and you decide how best to use the assets at hand, as well as what must be sacrificed.

Then you go for it; you pursue your dream living within your means, doing what must be done as it needs to be done (one step at a time, one hurdle at a time, moving forward as best you can focusing on your goal).

Sometimes, during the pursuit, fate intervenes and for whatever the reason (life altering encounter / circumstance, adversity), a greater passion is discovered, and a new dream is born. So you do what you must; evaluate, plan, decide, then act (living within your means).

Add to the picture a significant other, a family, a community, a town, a State, OUR Nation, and a dream of not one but many is

3

also possible (History has proven it; "WE the People . . .", OUR Nation exists). The whole process is consistent but; "compromise" is a necessity because no longer is it a dream of one, but more than one, sometimes many. Ultimately, the compromises made, were made out of necessity to "live within the means" to achieve the dream!

Was not "Freedom", "the birth of OUR Nation, "the evolution of our families, OUR society, OUR Nation" worth the sacrifices that were made on OUR behalf? Of course they were! As are the sacrifices made daily by each and every one of US pursuing our dream!

Success is directly dependent upon the fundamental principle of "living within your means".

No one's best interest is ever served, if we (as individuals or as a group), allow ourselves to believe or be led to believe that "living beyond our means is sustainable"!

It's not!!! History has proven that over, and over, and over again!

Find YOUR passion, dare to dream, evaluate, plan, decide, act, move forward "living within YOUR means".

Let US embrace and advance the dream of not one, but many, FREEDOM, by exercising the right to pursue that which WE dare to dream and are passionate about, while "living within OUR means". Let OUR example inspire and light the way for others.

I believe in YOU, I believe in ME, I believe in WE! Shall WE begin?

3. CAN ONE PERSON TRULY MAKE A DIFFERENCE?

Can one person truly make a difference?

Yes, One person can, and does make a difference!

The type of difference, and the extent of the difference is up to YOU, good or bad! The choice is YOURS to make!

This past Sunday, there were a couple of terrific stories in the Sunday NEWSDAY about people who chose to make a positive difference, and they were inspiring!

One article was entitled "Music to lift the older spirits", and it was about a young girl of 15, one of whom who had only been playing the piano for 2 years, witnessed something that (because of her love for music, particularly that of music played on the piano) disturbed her; she saw a baby grand piano go unused in a room full of people. At that moment, she lacked the confidence to get up in front of a room full of strangers, walk up to the piano, sit down, and start playing for the sole purpose of entertaining those present with music.

And yet, this then 15 year old went home and was moved within her heart to overcome her fear, and made a decision; she would return the following week with a friend to that same nursing home where she had seen the silent baby grand piano, and she would play for the benefit of others! Her name, Nikki Egna, from Port Washington, and she made a difference!

When she realized how much joy her playing brought to the elderly in the nursing home, she wanted to do more, and did, in a grand way! Over the next two year period, from when she was 15-17 years of age, she managed to recruit 75 fellow high school students who regularly perform music at senior living facilities, and six nursing homes around Long Island.

She formed "Piano for Patients", a registered non-profit with a goal to recruit 1,000 students and form partnerships with 150 facilities in the next couple of years. She actively recruits student volunteers from high school to become Location Leaders, who will then in turn recruit performers and promote Piano for Patients in their school, and organize performances at a variety of facilities. The organization I growing, and along with it, a scholarship and awards program as well for eligible participants. Her ultimate goal is to make this a Nationwide organization, and as participants graduate high school, and move on to college, they continue to participate there as well.

Can YOU imagine, think of the sheer number of lives that have benefited already from this young lady's desire to play music for the elderly; students, parents, teachers, school administrators, the elderly, etc. What a truly wonderful and remarkable thing, and each day more joy is spread! Well worth checking out more detail at pianoforpatients.org, especially if YOU would like to share your talents and make people feel good!

To think, it started with but one teen on one piano! Be inspired!

I had mentioned two, so here's the other; "The art of healing", also appeared in Sunday's NEWSDAY, about another person who had a talent and a vision to share her talent for the benefit of others. Her talent was art, her name Heather Buggee. An artist, she founded "Splashes of Hope" in 1996, a nonprofit organization whose mission is to transform ordinary hospitals, medical and social service facilities through custom art. Walls that once were stark, that depressed those stricken and battling illness, now are vibrant, full of color, life, and signal HOPE for the stricken.

Many lives have been brightened with these works of art, all done by people with similar interest, but inspired by Heather to get involved!

CAN ONE PERSON MAKE A DIFFERENCE, CAN YOU BE THAT ONE PERSON THAT MAKES A DIFFERENCE?

Of course YOU CAN!!!!!

I love the quote that was in the article about Heather, as related to the significance of one person making a difference; "I am only one, but still I am one. I cannot do everything, but still I can do something; and because I cannot do everything, I will not refuse to do the something that I can do."—words of Edward Everett Hale

WE are all significant, each and every one of US has a purpose. Look within YOUR mind, YOUR heart, and find YOUR PASSION, and pursue it relentlessly. Dare to be different, dare to be true, dare to be bold, DARE TO BE YOU! For OUR World, will be all the better for it!

Shall WE begin?

4. THE POWER OF ONE

One can make a difference; one person, one thought, one action.
Even the longest journey begins with but one step, followed by
another, and then another, and then another.

Every single one of US is significant, doe have purpose. When we
look within our mind, and our heart, when we find that which we
passionate about and pursue it fully, amazing things happen!

If YOUR passion is to teach, teach. If it is to sing, sing. If it is to
write, write. Whatever YOUR passion, be true to it, develop it,
master it, share it with the World and bear witness to "the power of
one".

And when those of similar passion are drawn to YOU, embrace
them, feel the strength of unity, of purpose, pursue it!

Have YOU not made a difference? Of course YOU HAVE, it starts
with but one!

Now is the time, today is the day, live it as it was meant to be lived,
fully!

5. HE REALIZED TRAVEL WASN'T JUST ABOUT ARRIVING AT THE DESTINATION . . .

Robert Moses had "the ability to get things done", and because of that, he was sought after time and time again. Before he was in the position as Chief of the New York State Park System, New York State had a very modest Parkland. By the time he was done, New York State had; 2,567,256 acres of Parkland, NYC had 658 playgrounds, 416 miles of parkways and 13 bridges were constructed creating Jones Beach State Park, the West Side Hwy in Manhattan, and the Long Island Parkway network. In addition, the Niagara and Saint Lawrence power projects were created and completed catapulting New York State to the top of the list as "the State to emulate", a state with cities that had Mass Transit, and the American Dream of the "open road" for traveling became a reality.

Now that didn't happen over night nor without the assistance of many talented and dedicated individuals that were inspired by his vision, and fed by his determination, "the ability to get things done". They weren't just hired, they signed on to be part of something much grander, they signed on to take a journey with him, one step at a time, and agreed to continue along the path less traveled until that path became OUR highway, literally!

The man wasn't even an engineer, he was well educated, self motivated, a man driven by his vision of "what could be", and would not stop until "it would be". His creation of a "Park at length, with a road running through it, allowing those from the city to travel distances surrounded by beauty while in the city, forever changed the face of many a city roadway, and Parkways were born to the delight of millions!

He realized it (travel), wasn't just about arriving at "the destination", there was much more to be enjoyed along the way, if only people had a reason to look! He gave them that reason!

And so it is for people as well; When we look within our mind and heart, find our passion and pursue it relentlessly, we discover our purpose, and then our real journey begins. One step, after another, we go on; encountering unexpected delights, maybe some hardships and headaches as well, but we can adapt, improvise, and find solutions allowing us to continue towards our destination / goal. We can enrich our lives, and the lives of most of those we encounter along the way if we "take notice", if we allow ourselves to look and see that which is around us.

When we get confused, side-tracked, lost or even seem to come to a dead end, we have the ability to reach out and ask for guidance or even for help if need be, to get us going in the right direction again, maybe the direction was actually more well defined as a result of our temporary setback.

The key for Robert Moses, as well as for each of us, is that we see a vision of where we want to go, what we want to be, what we want to do, and that will not happen unless we look within ourselves as often as it takes in mind and heart to discover / to find that which we are passionate about, and then have the resolve to pursue it relentlessly. Dare to be different, dare to be true, dare to be bold, dare to be you!

Our World is all the better for it, for each of us is significant! We come to know that as we travel our life's journey, if we take notice, if we look. How? By the strength we see in others when we inspire them by our example, by the strength we feel within ourselves when we allow others to inspire us at a time of crisis or loss of confidence. We come to know and trust ourselves, allowing us to believe, and by believing, we learn to have faith. As we continue our faith strengthens with each advancement, and we feel good, we see good, and we want others to feel good too. So, we grow, we reach out, spiritually, and physically.

Our belief, our FAITH takes on a whole new meaning; our passion and pursuit o purpose is of greater significance because we understand and come to accept that we all are significant. We realize that our purpose, our strength can be of assistance to others while they travel their journey, as theirs can be to us (especially during times of hardship or heartache) as we travel ours, we needn't be alone (nor would we be, if only we would see).

A perfect example, many are traveling their journey, and BAM, hardship, heartache finds them (say for instance, the passing of a loved one), what do they do? They take a detour, adapt, improvise, and in a manner of speaking, continue (for they are not where they were, they have traveled further).

And yet, their coming together during the time of hardship has allowed them all to be strengthened in ways they once were weak individually. That beloved sensation of strength new found and well received, ignites even greater passion, purpose, significance, and the drive and determination, "the ability to get things done", fans the fires of their FAITH, allowing all to move on, to continue on their journey, but now "knowing and believing" that they are not alone nor will they ever be, for they have learned to look, and now do see!

With FAITH all things are possible. Robert Moses had FAITH, and as a result, "the ability to get things done".

And such is my FAITH in GOD, in Country, in YOU; I believe in YOU, I believe in ME, I believe in WE! WE are all significant, each and every one, may WE all "be that which WE are meant to be". Then can each of US say; "I dared to be me, and that has made all the difference, WE are all significant!" Shall WE begin?

authorolearywrites
September 8, 2012

6. OUR MOST PRECIOUS RESOURCE

"The unanimous Declaration of the thirteen untied States of America.

When in the Course of human events, it becomes necessary for one people to dissolve the political bands which have connected them with another, and to assume among the powers of the earth, the separate and equal station to which the Laws of Nature and of Nature's God entitle them, a decent respect to the opinions of mankind requires that they should declare the causes which impel them to separation.

We hold these truths to be self-evident, that all men are created equal, that they are endowed by their Creator with certain unalienable Rights, that among these are Life, Liberty, and the pursuit of Happiness. That to secure these rights, Governments are instituted among Men, deriving their just powers from the consent of the governed . . ."

(excerpt from The Declaration of Independence)

With those words, and the rest of The Declaration, a Nation was born, OUR Nation, a Nation of "We the People".

"We the People of the United States, in Order to form a more perfect Union, establish Justice, insure domestic Tranquility, provide for common defense, promote the general Welfare, and secure the Blessings of Liberty to ourselves and our Posterity, do ordain and establish this Constitution for the United States of America."

(excerpt from The Constitution of The United States)

Times and technology change, names and places change, human nature does not! By knowing OUR History, and the History of other peoples, by learning OUR lessons well, WE have the opportunity to do more of what is right vs. what is wrong, more good vs. bad.

Many of us, starting form when we were little, think of History as boring, useless, dull! Nothing could be further from the truth, for History is LIFE, the LIFE of others, and there lies its greatest significance to those of us presently living; for human nature remains the same!

No matter what your interest, your passion, your desire, others of similar interest, passion, interests that have come before you, can afford you the greatest opportunity to learn and advance your progress, excel beyond even your previous thoughts or expectations by not repeating that which has failed in the past. For what is History but a story, a story of people with dreams, desires, wants, and needs, love, hate, power, greed, joy, triumph, tragedy, adversity, etc.

History is a story, not merely one, but millions. Millions of stories about people like you and I, many of whom had similar interest and expectations, and some were successful, some weren't. Can YOU imagine how fortunate YOU would be if by hearing even just one of their stories, you learned of something "not to do", and because YOU heard it first hand, the consequence of doing that which was done in that specific manner or at such a specific time or place was avoided!

Think of the love triangles that could have been avoided, the failed business attempts, the monumental school debt accumulated pursuing something you were not passionate about or interested in. Think about the romances near now near at hand, the business opportunities, the demand for the new product within your mind's eye, the passion burning as strong as the Sun from within your heart, heed their call armed with knowledge from lessons learned of those before YOU!

The elderly are OUR most precious resource, for aside from their many successes, even in their perceived failures, there is success of heart, of mind, of purpose when they share their story (their History) with US, and WE LISTEN!

If YOU were interested in business, would not YOU be a fool to miss the opportunity to hear Warren Buffet speak? Well believe you me, many of the elderly around YOU this day, over time, have acquired such precious and precise knowledge of YOUR similar interest, if only YOU were to ask to hear it, and then HEAR that which was being offered, a WEALTH beyond compare!

How fortunate can WE all be, if only WE learn to get OUR priorities right by learning! To learn well, one must have the right attitude towards learning, when enjoyable, its wonderful.

Why not approach the opportunity to learn for what it is, an opportunity to hear a unique story of that which was, of that which is, of that which can someday be if knowledge is gained, and applied with purpose coupled with passion! Let US seize the opportunity to benefit from the treasure that surrounds US all daily in every shape, size, and fashion imaginable by simply getting OUR priorities right and making the time now to learn from OUR most precious resource, OUR elders, for their time too, is finite (with end).

Their stories, their History (OUR History), is fascinating if ONLY WE HEAR, WE LISTEN, WE LEARN! Shall WE begin?

7.   FREEDOM—LET IT RING

Do words have power or do WE empower words?

". . . We hold these truths to be self evident, that all men are created equal, that they are endowed by their Creator with certain unalienable Rights, that among these are Life, Liberty, and the pursuit of Happiness. —That to secure these rights, Governments are instituted among Men, deriving their just powers from the consent of the governed. —That whenever any Form of Government becomes destructive of these ends, it is the Right of the People to alter or to abolish it, and to institute new Government, laying its foundation on such form, as to them shall seem most likely to effect their Safety and Happiness . . ." (from The Declaration of Independence in Congress July 4, 1776).

Freedom—Let Freedom ring!

Perhaps no word in the History of man has been more powerful, has stirred such heart felt emotion, has created bonds of unity amongst people of every race, religion, nationality as quickly or as completely as that one word; "FREEDOM".

People, like YOU and I, only here way before OUR time faced with oppression, intolerance, ridicule, hatred, violence, cruelty, injustice, embraced the meaning of that word, and empowered it with the belief of that which it represented to them, opportunity to be FREE, independent, to be equal in the eyes of their Creator.

No longer a mere word, it represented then, as it still does now, much, much more; a cause, a Right, an entitlement of "every person"—"equality", and with that equality, opportunity to make choices, to dream, and to pursue the dream.

Freedom—Let Freedom ring!

With the advance in technology, communication systems and networks allowing near instantaneous availability of that which is written, reported, documented, displayed in a variety of ways simultaneously, never before has that "Right", that entitlement of every person—"equality" been heard by the people of the World!

"FREEDOM"—"Freedom is ringing the World over, and its call is being heard within the hearts and minds of people, and they too now know of their Right of "equality" in the eyes of their Creator!

What price is "FREEDOM" worth; as History has shown, as daily events occur, as the future will demand, "FREEDOM" is worth every cost!

"FREEDOM"—"Let Freedom ring, hear its call, be not silent, stand, and be heard!" Equality is NOT for one, but for all, and that is worth everything! Be not silent, stand, and be heard, the World is listening!

Let the day come when all can share a common call; ". . . free at last, free at last, thank GOD we're free at last . . ." (Rev. Martin Luther King, Jr.).

"FREEDOM"—"It's time to answer, shall WE begin?

8. EVEN THE STRONG CAN BE WEAK

There are times when "even the strong can be weak", whether; physically, mentally, emotionally, spiritually. The causes, the circumstances can be as varied as the days on the calendar, and range from the trivial to life and death, but regardless, "even the strong can be weak".

Those that are physically strong, some as if with the strength to move mountains, can become powerless when they fail to believe the physical task at hand is within their capability to accomplish, so they don't even begin!

Those mentally strong, often take on Herculean tasks, achieving remarkable results, but they too, sometimes can be in capacitated when they fail to believe in that which they are capable of accomplishing!

Those emotionally strong often seem to become the compass from which the emotionally weak find some sense of direction and regain their footing, but when they (the emotionally strong), fall victim, and question their belief and ability to hold on, they too become emotionally weak, and it seems as if the whole World has near crumpled, and life as it was once known, will never be the same again!

Those that are spiritually strong, most often appear to be as if the bedrock upon which all others are sure strength and purpose can be found, regained, shared. When they become weak, the cause is most often so tragic and personal in nature, that the fire of Faith, of Belief, of HOPE, appears as if extinguished from within their very SOUL, and all OUR World appears to be dealt a devastating blow so severe in nature, that many find themselves questioning GOD directly with their own mouth; "God, how could YOU let this happen to one so firm in FAITH, in BELIEF in YOU, one with such HOPE in that which YOU are capable of doing?" To bear witness to the spiritual strong crumpled and crippled beyond a point of possible repair, is to experience; a tragedy of epic proportions that consumes and sucks the LIFE out of all that live, and the appearance of the triumph of evil over good.

What's the point, what does all this mean, what does it matter; to YOU, to me, to the WORLD in which WE are a part?

It's a refresher course in LIFE, and a reminder to US all, that; WE are human, not GOD, not GOD-like, and WE are not perfect. WE have strengths, and WE have weaknesses, and every day WE open OUR eyes, WE have a choice! No matter what hand WE are dealt, no matter what OUR circumstance, WE can CHOOSE what WE will do next!

WE can choose to become physically stronger! WE can choose to become mentally stronger! WE can choose to become emotionally stronger! WE can choose to become spiritually stronger! Yes, when the choices are made, action must follow (that too is a choice, one that needs to be taken)! And YES, for some, becoming stronger in any or all of the above will require serious effect, and sacrifice.

Can YOU imagine how much better OUR WORLD would be? I CAN! The choice is OURS to make!

When WE just had the huge Snowstorm in the Northeast, my town of Holtsville in Brookhaven Township, Suffolk County, Long Island, New York, had an average of 24-27 inches of snow that appeared as if dumped by Nature's trucks in a blink of an eye. Our family lives on a double sided court off another residential street (if you picture a dog bone suspended horizontally in the middle by a string, and the string was the access road from another residential street, and the bone was our double sided court, you would have a good visual grasp of where we live, and would understand how our block would be one of the very last blocks "ever" to be plowed on a good day).

In blizzard conditions, and without leadership present in Brookhaven Township, one of Suffolk County's largest Townships became paralyzed, with cars and people in cars stranded within sight of mega shopping malls and thousands of homes, some were stranded for more than 12 hours. The TV images of snowbound cars on major roadways made your blood boil. These cars, and the people in them, weren't stranded on remote interstates, they were on major "local" rods in densely populated areas that pay huge taxes for services to be rendered when and if needed (from clearing roads, to rescue, if need be).

"The system" didn't fail them, didn't fail US, PEOPLE DID, by the choices they made (all documented now by I'm sure almost every newspaper and news organization in this region as to "how NOT to handle a snowstorm).

Well, I, my sons, and many of our neighbors, as well as from blocks all over, made better choices, and got busy. We went out, hour after hour, and dug our way out from our houses, our driveways, our roads using shovels, snow blowers, ice scrapers, focusing on the goal at hand until it was met, then the next, and the next. WE dug out cars as WE came to them, moving tons and tons of snow with shovels, ice scrapers, snow blowers, and all the while, WE demonstrated to OUR youth how powerful choice can be, and of what consequence. They learned how powerful and significant one could be, especially if and when joined by another of whom was focused upon a similar goal!

Amongst US all, there were those physically strong, others mentally strong, some emotionally strong, but the strongest by far amongst US all, were the Spiritually strong, for they would not let US fail, and so when the plows did come (days later), they connected plowed streets to OUR dug out streets that OUR vehicles had already traveled upon.

Each of US, made a choice to NOT accept that which WE had been dealt, but chose to do that which was better, and better did WE do!

The strengths of many, empowered all of US to be greater than any one of US! Success was OURS!

Now, with that Storm gone, there is more for all of US to do, IF WE SO CHOOSE!

Dare to be different, dare to be true, dare to be bold, dare to be YOU! The choice is OURS to make, shall WE begin?

9. YOUR TIME HAS COME, IS NOT OUR WORLD ALL THE BETTER FOR IT?

On the last day of each year, I count my blessings and give thanks for how very fortunate I have been, and pray for strength and guidance to do better, to be better in the coming new year!

This year, I felt an urgency to share that which I felt with family, with friend. I don't know why the sense of urgency was so strong, but I have learned that when such things happened in my life, there proved to be a pretty good, and timely reason, later!

So, on the last day of this year, while commuting to NYC via train, I fired off text messages to immediate family listing my blessings with regard to each individual family member, and sent them (keep in mind it was 4:08 am EST, and they were all sleeping). No sooner had I sent them, than I was richly rewarded with their unexpected responses, responses that brought great joy to my heart.

So, as my last day of 2012 progressed at work, I delighted in the knowledge that my written words had touched all their hearts, as had their presence in my life touched mine! For you see, for me, it is with written words that I have found my voice, my means to communicate best that which is within me!

What's YOURS? Is it speaking, music, art, building, creating, through YOUR hands? How best is it for YOU to communicate that which YOU feel?

Why do I ask this of YOU, and what does it have to do with what's above? I'll tell YOU!

Clearly, the joy that my words gave them (my family), and the joy their responses gave me, enriched us all!

Because of that, I became anxious for YOU to also be able to start
the New Year with such JOY, JOY unique to YOU, your family,
your friends, in a manner, and by means best suited for each of
YOU.

For you see, although the way WE communicate to OUR families
and friends what our blessings are, what WE are thankful for in
different ways and means, WE are acknowledging that for which,
and how for which, WE have been blessed. By doing that, WE
honor GOD in Heaven, WE have reason to give thanks, and each of
US has the opportunity to seek guidance, and to praise GOD in a
manner most natural and real to US.

My greatest blessing has been my FAITH, and my BELIEF in
GOD, because no matter whatever happened, no matter what road I
traveled, what hardship endured, "I knew" I would be blessed with
a wife, and children (I knew it within my heart, within my Soul).
For "that wife" to be my wife Diane, and "those children" to be
my Step-son Joe, Michael, and Anna, and their significant others
to be Theresa (with Joe), Michelle (with Michael), and Danny (with
Anna), just made it all more perfect, with a wealth beyond my
wildest expectations! To be able to share how blessed I had been
with them by means most suitable to me, written word, and know
that brought them joy, was priceless!

Such is my sincerest, and greatest wish for each and all of YOU,
that YOU come to have such FAITH, such BELIEF in GOD that
as YOU travel YOUR life's journey, YOU TOO, will be blessed
with; that which is within YOUR heart, that YOU will realize how
blessed YOU are, that YOU will share how YOU have been blessed
and give thanks, that YOU will bring joy to the hearts of those
YOU love, and by so doing, YOU will be rewarded with the joy
they return to YOUR heart. All this I hope and pray YOU do and
experience in the manner that suits YOU!

For each and every one of US is significant, has a passion, a
purpose, and when it is found within our mind and heart, pursued
relentlessly, it is All of US that benefits, as does OUR World! Have

FAITH, BELIEVE, ask for guidance knowing and believing in YOUR heart and Soul that WE are NOT alone nor will WE ever be!

Dare to be YOU, dream, BELIEVE, DO! If YOU do that which YOU are capable of doing, are not YOU significant? If I do what I am capable of doing, am I not significant? If that which WE do is significant, and WE do it, is not OUR World the better for it? Of course it is! WE CAN DO BETTER!

Many have not FAITH, have not BELIEF, but ALL have within them the desire, for IT is within US all, as will HE be if ONLY HE is asked! HE will feed that desire, your FAITH and BELIEF in HIM will show YOU the way! YOUR Blessings will be many, YOUR wealth beyond compare, it's a new day, a new year, YOUR time has come, stand, let YOUR VOICE be heard!

I believe in YOU, I believe in ME, I believe in WE, and I know WE WILL DO BETTER! Shall WE begin?

10. WE HOLD THIS TRUTH TO BE SELF EVIDENT, WE CAN DO BETTER!

To my fellow Americans, especially those affected by Hurricane / Tropical Storm Sandy; My thoughts and prayers are with each and every one of YOU. I am no stranger to heartache and sorrow, to utter and complete destruction, injury, and death nor to the accompanying sense of hopelessness, fright, despair, sadness, frustration, and ultimately anger at the World as it seems to pass the stricken by as if not to notice or care!

At such times and moments like this, the shear magnitude of the destruction, the millions of lives turned upside down in what seems as if the blink of an eye, feels as crushing to OUR spirit and Soul as if the weight of collapsed concrete flattening our body inch by inch with no end in sight until no life remains within us.

This I say to YOU, this I yell to YOU, this I swear to YOU; "HOLD ON, HOLD ON, HELP IS COMING, have FAITH, and BELIEVE, HELP IS COMING!" And until it gets there, look within yourself and decide to survive, to fight the odds that seem so daunting, and take action; one step, then another, then another, then another.

As you move forward, grab hold of your loved one, your family member, your friend, your neighbor, and turn them to move forward with YOU; one step, then another, then another, then another.

History has shown US all, time and time again, the brilliance, the magnificence, the extraordinary ability that is within each of US yearning to be let loose at times such as these, and once unleashed, the results often surpass even the grandest expectations!

From amidst the wreckage, dare to be YOU, let YOUR creative genius find that which can be made a useful tool to assist YOU in moving one step forward, then keep going one step, then another, one task, then another. Focus on "the next step / the next task" and complete it! Then move as I know YOU can, for I BELIEVE in YOU! YOUR family, YOUR friends, YOUR neighbors BELIEVE in YOU!

At this particular moment, so many people are looking in so many directions, at so many tasks, that a shared vision of that which can be accomplished / that should be accomplished appears lost, absent.

The resources available to each of US, and all of US, are beyond any one person's comprehension if focus is not first found (too much too soon, all at once is overwhelming). Once a priority is found, focus found, resources can be mustered / marshaled, a plan devised, action taken, goals accomplished.

The logistics capabilities of the United States are unmatched by any other Nation in the World, and the resolve of "WE the People" to accomplish that which WE set OUR sights on, is second to none!

Food, clothing, shelter, accompanied with the resolve and determination that WE can and will do better this time, will create an aire of expectation that success will be imminent, and it will be, for failure is NOT an option!

Now is the time for action, get up, get on YOUR feet, and take one step, then another. Reach out and help another stand on their feet, and then take another step together, then another.

WE can do better, and from this devastation WE have been given the opportunity to do better. NOW is the time, so HOLD ON, and get BUSY, YOUR time is now, OUR time is now!

I believe in YOU, I believe in ME, I believe in WE, and WE CAN DO BETTER! Shall WE begin?

11. A SPECIAL REQUEST TO THE YOUTH OF AMERICA . . .

A special request to the youth of America, as well as the youth of the World, for YOU are "OUR" future; This massive super storm (Sandy), that is now bearing down on the East Coast of America will cause catastrophic destruction, loss of life, and unparalleled opportunity for YOU to truly change "OUR WORLD".

How? Because of your youth, your imagination, your creativity, your enthusiasm, your passion, because of the feelings you will experience as a result of how this storm impacted OUR families, OUR friends, OUR neighbors, OUR communities, towns, states, Nation. It is your youth and your nature to challenge, to question, to learn, to seek answers, and take risks.

Some of the greatest advancements to all fields of study, improvements to the way WE communicate, manufacture, travel, calculate have been directly advanced by those of similar youth that have come before YOU, youth that would not or could not accept that a "better way, a better product, a better service" was not possible.

To YOU, the Future of OUR WORLD, to YOU of whom pockets of change are at times a luxury, and who understand the significance of an increase of cents to the percentage of your student loans, pennies can, over time become monumental, YOU can value the significance of saving / reducing expenses of essential and necessary products and services that directly impact the quality of OUR lives. YOU can clearly, and easily picture yourself finding a better use for $15.00 of every $100.00 spent on powering OUR homes, businesses, electronic devices. YOU can value the significance of when the traditional power grids fail for whatever the reason (as in this case, this super storm), being able to turn to

26

the shear power of the destructive force of the storm into "a means" of creating power to facilitate a more timely and efficient recovery.

When satellite dishes were first introduced to home rooftops, they were hated, laughed at, called eye soars. But they brought a new way, competition, an alternative, their mere presence made everyone else become more creative, more efficient, and methods more cost efficient as well. Well dishes are now so an acceptable sight, that people often don't even notice them.

Solar and wind technology has advanced in leaps and bounds, but yet their use is met with great resistance for a variety of reasons, some valid, most not! As you watch the fury of this storm, think of this; with every blow of the wind We could be creating electricity in each and every home and business, no matter rain or snow accompanying it. WE could be storing it for use when and if needed (like when the power grids fail, falling trees ripe lines down, equipment is destroyed).

As you view the millions of homes that will, shortly be without power, some for days / maybe weeks, think of how valuable an asset a wind turbine the size of a satellite dish could've been on each and every home, and business, capable of producing 15% of the electricity used by that house or business (and those are the small wind systems available right now, already, without YOUR focus and imagination).

Think of when the storm passes, as all storms do at some point, and the wind subsides, the Sun comes out, so the Solar system now uses the light from the Sun to produce the same 15% of electricity used by each house or business for that same purpose. Many people picture ugly huge panels visible from the street, as unacceptable eye-soars, well guess what? For years now, some builders have already been installing roof shingles on houses that take the place of those ugly panels, capable of collecting and using that which the Sun so generously offers. They simply need to be hooked up to the rest of the solar system equipment when the home owner decides to go solar (the builders were slick, they know the shingles are already installed, so when they get the call to install solar to that house, they charge for labor that has already been paid for when the house was constructed and first purchased, the hardware, batteries, converters, and some additional wiring is all that's actually being added). But the main point is this, solar technology has advanced in leaps already, and those huge panels are no longer the only way to go, you've probably been looking at houses with solar roof shingles already installed in some of your neighborhoods for years and just assumed they were regular roof shingles (no eye-soar present).

Bottom-line, WE have had, do have right now, the capability for every single home old and new, and for every business, to create and use a minimum of 15% of their power during such catastrophic times such as this. Think about that when YOU attempt to take a hot shower tomorrow and can't, when you attempt to blow dry your hair and can't, when you attempt to make your morning coffee and can't, when you attempt to recharge your electronic devices and can't. Not to mention that 15% of every $100.00 spent on electricity by every single household and business could be spent on something more productive or useful to the family or business.

YOU, the YOUTH of WE, the YOUTH of OUR WORLD are OUR CHANGE; YOUR voices should be thundering across OUR NATIONS demanding solar and wind be instilled in every new construction, as well as in everything that is reconstructed after such storms pass! Why? Because it's the right thing to do, by volume the costs would come down, the savings go up, and the savings could be used to fund even better advancements in many areas, and to help jump start markets, economies, subsidize programs, help people.

YOU are the power empowering that which will be, YOU are significant!

DARE TO BE YOU!

I believe in YOU, I believe in ME, I believe in WE! WE CAN DO BETTER! Shall WE begin?

12. SIMPLY DO YOUR BEST

While commuting home this evening on a packed Long Island Railroad train from New York City to Ronkonkoma, Long Island, I could not help hearing multiple conversations about the Presidential debates, the state of OUR economy, and another failed terrorist attack in lower Manhattan, this one by the New York Federal Reserve Bank.

Rightfully so, the topics were and should be of concern to all of US, especially as WE near Election Day! The strength of any democracy is directly reliant upon the People of that democracy participating. And to participate, YOU, WE need to be informed.

It was quite inspiring to hear how passionately people were experiencing themselves, although a few seemed to be of the mind that what they said or what they did was or would be of no consequence! I disagree, because there is always a consequence to each decision, each action or lack of action any of US takes.

If each of US is serious about turning the economy around, here's a simple step in the right direction WE can all take each day starting right this moment with ourselves; Decide to do "your best" at each thing you do during the course of your day, in each and everything simply do "your best". From crunching numbers, to folding laundry, to getting mail from the mailbox, simply do "YOUR BEST"!

So you may stink at folding clothes, but folding them to the "best you can" helps to set your mind and your attitude in the right direction. Doing your job, balancing your family budget, coaching your children's team, singing in your church's choir, painting your apartment, answering your telephone to the "best of your ability" reflects within your tone, your body language, your manner, your attitude, and draws others to you.

You inspire others to want to be more like that, people start to feel better about themselves, about what they can do, about what they will do! Enthusiasm spreads, participation increases, people are more industrious, production increases, more goods and services are purchased.

Confidence and appreciation grows, dreams are dreamt and pursued, all while we are "simply doing our individual best". The air becomes electrified with infinite possibilities all because WE, first as individuals, then as a People, decided to "simply do OUR best".

Don't procrastinate, decide right now to "simply do your best" in everything you do, and do it! You'll be AMAZED at the results, and so very inspired to want others to feel it, see it, and experience as well!

Aren't YOU worth it, don't YOU deserve to feel good, don't YOU want YOUR family to feel good? Of course YOU do! So what are YOU waiting for, the decision is YOURS TO MAKE!

MAKE IT, "simply do your best"!

I believe in YOU, I believe in ME, I believe in "WE the People", and WE are going to do better! Shall WE begin?

13. CONSEQUENCES

CONSEQUENCES, there are always consequences to every decision made, every action taken or not taken. One need NOT live YOUR LIFE frozen in fear of possible consequences (". . . what if this happens or that happens?"), but it would be in YOUR BEST INTEREST, to seriously think things through mindful and respectful of "that" which "may result" of a decision "YOU" make today, and the action taken or inaction.

No one can escape the CONSEQUENCES of that which will occur once a decision is made and implemented, but they must be dealt with, one way or another!

Although each of US is unique, human nature is pretty consistent and has remained so throughout most of recorded time, as is evidenced when History is studied.

So, when WE study History (our families, our friends, OUR Nations), when WE speak with people and hear of THEIR experiences, often WE can better anticipate CONSEQUENCES of OUR decisions that WE might not have been mindful of, yet! So, "maybe" WE could benefit by that which was learned, and make a better decision for ourselves, and our future.

Wouldn't THAT possibility be a worthy investment of our time and effort? Of course it would!!!!

How many a LOVE story are without imperfection, without hurt or sorrow, joy and jubilation, sainthood or martyrdom? And yet, is not LOVE or even the possibility of it, a worthy investment of our time and effort? Of course it is!!!!

CONSEQUENCES BE THEY MAY, ". . . to be or not to be . . .",
the choice is YOURS alone to make. ARE YOU NOT WORTHY
OF YOUR TIME AND YOUR EFFORT?

OF COURSE "YOU" ARE, AS ARE "WE" ALL!!!! Shall not
TRUE LOVE be given a chance?

What say YOU? Is not NOW as good as time as any to begin? Have
FAITH, BELIEVE, dare to be YOU, for YOU are magnificent!
This is YOUR defining moment, an opportunity to awaken that
which has been within YOU. Heed its call, this is YOUR time, for
YOU ARE WORTHY OF THE TIME AND THE EFFORT, and
OUR World will benefit as well!

Shall WE begin?

14. ONE OF LIFE'S GREATEST REWARDS . . .

One of Life's greatest rewards, is the realization and the knowledge within YOUR mind and heart, that YOU have been of positive influence on another, that YOU have brightened another person's day, encouraged them, inspired them, given them cause to smile.

How truly magnificent, and yet humbling is that realization and that knowledge, for it is at that moment that YOU understand the significance of YOUR being; "YOU have made a difference in the LIFE of another, and in so doing, a grand difference has been made within YOUR LIFE as well"!

"YOU DARED TO BE YOU, AND OUR WORLD HAS BEEN BLESSED WITH A DIFFERENCE, FOR YOU ARE SIGNIFICANT!"

Such a reward comes from but one being, GOD! Does not a Parent know such reward when looking into the eyes of their child? Does not a Teacher know of such reward when their student completes that which has been taught successfully? Is not any Professional so rewarded when they have completed that which they are so trained to do successfully, and their Family, Friend, Client, Associate sings praise with but a smile and warmth of heart?

So very rich are WE, if only WE allow OURSELVES to SEE; Surrender YOURSELF to that which YOU were meant to be, YOU!!!

Dare to be different, dare to be true, dare to be bold, DARE TO BE YOU! For YOU are MAGNIFICENT! A gift are WE ALL to the World in which WE live. Our World benefits, as it should, when

WE are that which WE are meant to be, OURSELVES (for as long as WE are allowed to walk this Earth)!

So look within YOUR MIND and HEART, find YOUR PASSION and pursue it relentlessly, DARE TO BE YOU!

Live YOUR Life as YOU were meant to live it, by BEING YOU!!! Take the DARE, DARE TO BE YOU!

For the DAY will come, when YOU TOO shall feel the reward from within, and feel like shouting with joy; "I DARED TO BE ME, AND IN OUR WORLD HAVE I MADE A DIFFERENCE, AND SO SHALL "YOU", FOR "YOU TOO" ARE AS SIGNIFICANT! Shall WE begin?

15. IF NOT YET BUT BY THE GRACE OF GOD . . .

I have often heard it said that; ". . . God does not give us more than we are capable to deal with . . .". Equally, if not more often, I've heard it said that; ". . . God has given all humans the Freedom of Choice . . .".

But along with that Freedom of Choice comes consequence; right or wrong, justice or injustice, good or evil, happiness or sadness, wealth or poverty, feast or famine, love or hatred, acceptance or denial, trust or betrayal, optimism or pessimism, complexity or simplicity, to "live" your life or "die" while living, to lead or to follow, to serve and protect or abuse and exploit, to participate or to stand on the sideline, to seek solutions or add to the problems, to find and fulfill your destiny or deny it.

For every single one of US is significant, is unique, and has a purpose. Fortunate is the person who chooses to look within mind and heart to find their purpose, realize it, pursue it, and fulfills it. Unfortunate is the person who chooses to ignore their gift, their purpose, that which is unique unto them, especially if they ignored it out of fear.

Our lives here on Earth are finite, with end, some much shorter than others. The minutes of our life's journey are precious, and because of that I honestly in my mind, my heart, and my Soul, that we are continually blessed along our way by the Grace of God by those we meet, the encounters and experiences we share, the events we witness.

As parents, teachers, coaches, brothers, sisters, friends, neighbors, mentors, managers, leaders in every field and endeavor, it benefits all of us to promote belief; belief in one's self, belief in that which is unique unto another, belief in that which might be.

For with that belief in self, in another, in others, in shared vision, comes faith. With belief and faith fanning the fires of purpose within our minds and hearts, fear of trying, fear of comment, fear of failure has no home nor strength because failure is not an option. Our blessings encountered along our journey become recognized, and strengthen our belief, our faith, and drive us on allowing our precious finite minutes to not just be used, but experienced in their glory.

How could WE; as individuals, as a People, as the Peoples of this World not benefit? WE would! It's never too late as long as the air flows through our nose or our mouth (our minutes are not up).

Let us see our children for who they are by encouraging them to be that which they can be, to do that which they can do. Believe in them, so they can believe too. Have faith in them, encourage them, inspire them.

Let our children see us believing in ourselves, pursuing our purpose, allowing them to believe in us, allowing them to understand how similar yet unique each one of us is. For then, can they begin to understand, and appreciate the blessings of so many. With such knowledge, belief, faith, purpose recognized, destiny can be fulfilled!

If not yet but by the Grace of God, our life's journey's lessons and blessings never would've been learned nor purpose recognized. Destiny denied, true tragedy of epic proportion.

Let the importance of having belief and faith be held true, for it's God's Grace for me and YOU! OUR journey calls, shall WE begin?

16. HEALING HANDS; A WALK TO REMEMBER

Since last October, 2012, each workday I would spend close to 14 hours total on my feet. With each step of my right foot, pain would shoot through my entire leg to my hip / groin. Until this Sept, 2013, I was able to block the pain within my mind. Then no more, so I took an over the counter to help manage the pain.

Soon thereafter, I was given a date to correct the problem, Oct 7th surgery. Great, relief / an end in sight. Well, Sept. 26th came, and so did the realization I was having terrible trouble taking even one more step (although I did).

Well, my wife received a phone call that day, that due to an opening, my surgery was being moved up to Sept. 30th (one week earlier). Was not GOD'S HAND at work?

Were not the HEALING HANDS of my loving wife Diane, and my children, and my friends at work with their encouragement that within days an end would come? And that be so, was not HIS HAND at work as well?

Those last few days before surgery, my wife and my children saw me having my most difficult and most painful moments each time I just attempted to put on my right sock (sometimes it would take me 10-15 minutes).

Once surgery was done, new pieces placed within me, and I was awake out of recovery and up into my room, they (my wife and my sons), saw me stand on my right foot without pain, and take two steps! Were not the HEALING HANDS of the Surgeons, the Nurses, and their support team at work? And if that be so, was not HIS HAND at work as well?

When I arrived at the Rehab Facility, and while I was being evaluated so they could determine the best way to proceed, I relayed the story you read above, and; one of the first things one Occupational Therapist did was to run out to her office and get a device that assists a person when they have difficulty putting on socks. Right then, she taught me how to put my socks on using the device, and made sure I could put both on before leaving the room! Were not her HEALING HANDS at work? And if that be so, WAS NOT HIS HAND AT WORK AS WELL?

WE all have HEALING HANDS if WE hear that which is within OUR heart and choose to use them!

I have been blessed by many a HEALING HAND, and I thank GOD each day for those blessings, and through my words I pray maybe, my HEALING HANDS WILL reach out to YOU to have FAITH, to BELIEVE, to have HOPE, because WE are not alone!

DARE TO BE DIFFERENT, DARE TO BE TRUE, DARE TO BE BOLD, DARE TO BE YOU! YOU are significant, as are WE all! WE all have HANDS that can HEAL! Shall WE begin?

17. WHO ARE WE TO JUDGE?

Today, Whitney Houston is being laid to rest. At her funeral, there will be many that knew her, some very well, some not as well, and some that knew her only by her works and by what they were allowed to see and hear over the years.

Her death, her life are now being scrutinized by every form of media imaginable, officially and unofficially. Investigators are endlessly attempting to find anything that can be found. So, of course some darkness, some despair, some heartache, some trials and tribulations, factual and fantasy have come to be made more widely known.

Talk shows, news stories, everyday conversations have been dominated by Whitney's life, good and bad. Many people have opinions based upon what they have learned or chosen to learn, as how best to honor, remember, or say farewell to Whitney Houston.

One person, the Governor of New Jersey, decided to honor her by ordering the flags be flown at half staff. That decision, well intended, started a firestorm within the state, as well as across the Nation. Why? Because the lowering of the Nation's Flag has always been thought to be reserved as a sign of ultimate honor bestowed upon those that have served OUR Nation with honor (one article actually cited veterans and politicians "only" as deserving the honor, believe you me, I have known some of, and known of some in both of those categories that I would never want OUR Nation's Flag to be so lowered).

I have served with those that have Fallen in every branch of the service for OUR Nation, for some states, some cities, some towns. I have gone to bat for many a politician Nationally, locally. Some have passed, and the honor was allowed, some have passed and the honor was denied (the reasons as varied as your imagination). Rightly? Wrongly? Depends upon whom YOU ask, and when YOU ask them.

With regard to this particular person of interest, Whitney Houston, and at this particular moment in time, the controversy seems to center most strongly upon; 1) A person of undeniably GOD blessed talent, of whom at times succumbed to substance abuse (for whatever the reason), and was therefore deemed not a good role model, 2) She, Whitney, was not in the service of OUR NATION.

I believe every single one of US is significant, has a purpose, a reason for being, and when we (as individuals), finally look within mind and heart, discover that which we are passionately called upon to door be, pursue it relentlessly, we as individuals benefit, WE as a People, a Nation, OUR World, benefits, and WE honor OUR Father in Heaven by being and doing that which we were meant to be and do.

Does not a parent love their child, in sickness and in health? Does not a child love their parent as the parentis known, for that may be the only parent as known?

My Mother was an alcoholic (she didn't start out that way), and being the youngest, I thought I was the only one that knew. Never for one minute of any day did I ever feel threatened by her or not loved by her, she was my Mother, and I loved her with all my heart. I tried every possible way a kid to help her that I could think of. Little did I know at the time that substance abuse is "an illness". The family fractured, off to boarding school, then to college.

The years passed, as did my Mother (age 55), as a result of her illness. It was by her love and because of her illness I learned compassion (when I could've chosen anger and hatred), my FAITH became my rock upon which to plant my feet.

Whitney discovered her gift, her talent, her calling singing in church. She pursued it singing praise to GOD. Her words sung with the blessing of GOD above touched the hearts and minds of millions the World over. Who are WE to judge her? Did she not honor GOD in Heaven serving HIM, and in so doing, were not WE (the People of this Nation, in whom GOD do WE trust) served as well, and were not the People of World blessed by the Grace of GOD allowing her words, her music, HIS message to reach the hearts and minds of HIS children; "I will always love you . . ."?

Listen to Whitney sing that song, crank it up, and try to tell me to my face that YOU have NOT been touched by the HAND of GOD, that YOU did NOT feel a tingling within YOUR Soul, a gentle blessing upon YOUR head telling YOU to go on, to have FAITH, to BELIEVE, to fear not because YOU, ME, WE, are not alone nor will WE ever be alone!

From this one that has served, knowing intimately the sacrifices, the pain, the suffering, the love, and the honor of the Fallen, and fulfilling that calling, that purpose within my mind and my heart "to write words to be of positive influence" I write; "Whitney, OUR Flag is at half staff in my mind and my heart to honor YOU, for YOU have served US well, and in so doing YOU honored OUR FATHER in HEAVEN."

There is no doubt in my mind or in my heart where Whitney is, she is singing in the chorus of Angels the words of OUR FATHER, "I will always love you . . ."! And for that I say thank-you!

18. "I'VE GOT TO FEED MY BABIES"

The young Mother of three; one son 12, one son 1 yr 4 months, and one daughter less than a week old could not help feeling a bit overwhelmed and pissed off at her husband, he had gone off to work as if it was just another day. She had only been home from the hospital one day since giving birth to their daughter via cesarean section. Yes, she had been in the hospital for a few days, but that didn't change the fact that she had been opened up for the second time in less than 2 years to give "them" another child.

And now, here she was, "alone" with three children that she did love dearly, all requiring; attention, feeding, cleaning, clothing, teaching, playing, hugging, picking up, carrying, putting down, amusing, never abusing, getting to the bus, going to doctor appointments, shopping, doing endless laundry, all while maintaining a clean and healthy home. "A bit overwhelmed and pissed off" at her husband sure sounds justified and warranted under those circumstances. How in his right mind could he possibly expect her to do all those things she did, so wonderfully, so lovingly, not doubting for a second that they would be done, when she was in a such weakened state?

The answer was simple, the guy, her husband, was clueless (aren't most?), and had not learned the lesson he needed to learn the first time his wife had come home after her first cesarean section. For he had done the same thing then, a day after she had come home with "their child", he had gone off to work as if it was just another day.

It must be said; that she, this magnificent woman, Mother, Wife, never complained nor failed to carry-out any task. The children were well loved, well cared for, the house well maintained, a warm and loving home, because of her.

The husband did do things "he believed" (as I am sure most husbands do), a husband was supposed to do, when they were supposed to be done, but he missed the mark, and remained clueless about some of the things that were monumental to his Wife (and I'm sure to most others as well). So, naturally, but never with intent, he hurt her (as I'm sure many a husband do without intent), he hurt her heart! Wounded, she carried on without complaint.

The years passed, and the husband was hurt in an accident at work; a hernia (his first), requiring surgery right away. Surgery done, home the same day, the husband was in pain, and scheduled "not to go back to work, manual labor (at that time he worked a plumbing supply house where the movement of boilers was done many times in a day) for 4 weeks. So, there he was, home, in bed, thinking he was going to be pampered to for 4 weeks. Guess what, that wasn't going to happen, pay-back time! "GET UP, GET BUSY, YOU HAVE CHORES TO DO, and KIDS TO TAKE CARE OF." With reluctance, with complaint, moaning and groaning he did the minimum he could get away with (what a wimp), never overly thankful or appreciative of all that his wife was doing for him, even then (what a clueless ass). He missed the opportunity to have truly learned a great, great lesson about life, about love, about teamwork, about caring, about sharing! He blew it again!

And how did she, this magnificent woman, Mother, Wife, that never complained nor failed to carry-out any task respond after being wounded again; "she carried on" with a grace and beauty that he was still too blind to fully see and in a manner that would please her.

More years passed, kids now fully grown, and magnificent and loving in their own right, their Mother has done them right always, taught them well, guided them, inspired them, demanded of them, and loved them with all her heart.

Opportunity knocked once more, another injury almost identical to his first one caused the husband to have surgery again, only this time his eyes had learned to see, his heart had truly learned to feel. His FAITH, and his BELIEF had finally, finally brought him HOME to love and appreciate this magnificent woman, Mother, Wife, and their extended family of fully grown, magnificent and loving children.

The woman; My Wife, Diane, my love like no other!

And this I pray and wish for YOU; May your FAITH, and your BELIEF allow your eyes and your heart to always truly see, the beauty, the grace, the love, bestowed upon thee! Today is the first day of the rest of your life, the choice is yours to make how and with whom you will live it! Have FAITH, Believe, YOU are not alone nor will YOU ever be!

19. IF BY CHANCE YOU HAPPEN TO SEE A BUTTERFLY OR TWO . . .

Whenever I can, I go to the Ecology Site to walk the perimeter path. It affords me the opportunity to "slow down" and to take notice of that which I have, that which I can see, and that which I love to dream! These days, I'm re-teaching myself how to walk correctly (I had surgery a couple of weeks ago that corrected an ailment, a hernia, and until it was corrected, I hadn't realized how much I had changed how I walked out of necessity to minimize pain).

So, with great enthusiasm I hit the path at a turtle's pace and set my goal for two times around (at this rate I'll be in the Olympics in 40 years or so).

As I rounded the first bend, there before me, there had to be between 30-40 white butterflies, it was magnificent to see in the early morning light! I have been told in the past by someone who is an authority on the subject, that butterflies are Souls set free that have chosen to stay here to be of assistance to others in need. Think about that for a minute; picture the butterflies flying carefree as if dancing in the morning light, and while your marveling at their magnificence, you remember what you had been told. If you believed what you had been told, that would mean that there before you, were 30-40 Souls that were there to assist YOU. Can YOU imagine how YOU would feel? The sheer joy, the excitement? Now multiply that by ten and you'll know how I felt at that moment!

You see, I believe what I was told, and believe you me, YOU would too!

During my entire walk around the path both times, there was at least one or more butterflies visible to me. I could not take my eyes off them or marvel more at their magnificence in their simplicity.

As a result, I finished my walk so refreshed, so happy, feeling so well blessed! What a terrific way to start the day! How could I not give thanks to the Lord above!

So this I say to you, in the course of your days, whether at work, home or play, allow yourself to see that which is around you, "slow down" even if but for a few precise minutes and take notice of that which is around you. If by chance you happen to see a butterfly or two, BELIEVE it was not by chance, it was by design, and THEY are there FOR YOU!

WE are not alone nor will WE ever be! BELIEVE! Today is the first day of the rest of OUR lives, let US choose to LIVE IT as WE were meant to!

I believe in YOU, I believe in ME, I believe in WE! Shall WE begin?

20. "LOOK MOMMY, AREN'T THE FLOWERS BEAUTIFUL?" TO WHICH THE MOTHER REPLIED;

The little girl was probably 5 or 6 years old, and could not have been more adorable when she called to her Mother; "Look Mommy, aren't the flowers beautiful?" To which the Mother replied; "Oh my, they are very beautiful! Would you like to pick them and take them home?" The little girl smiled a smile that would warm the coldest heart, and answered . . .

I awoke to a gorgeous morning, cool temp, clear sky, slight breeze, and a magnificent Sunrise. I showered, shaved, got dressed, ate, grabbed a bottle of water, and was out the door in record time (for someone recovering from recent surgery). I was anxious to get to the Town's Ecology Site so I could walk the perimeter path, I'm in the process of teaching myself how to walk correctly again (my ailment, hernia, that required surgery in June 2012 to fix, over time had caused me to walk differently to ease the pain).

As I pulled into the Ecology Site, I marveled at the beauty; with the previous day's rains behind us, everything was lush, and all the colors were popping out in the morning light. It seemed as if there were 40 shades of green, reds, and yellows, pinks, and purples, blues, and white, just truly magnificent!

Ever so enthused, out I went, taking it all in, while I thanked God above for all my many blessings, and for allowing me to be here on such a fine day! As I continued along the path, it was amazing to see how much life was all around me, and how much was escaping the consciousness of those running, walking, biking as they zoomed passed me.

I almost wanted to say; "Slow down, don't you see, the beauty and the grace bestowed upon thee?" But I didn't, because I knew they were there for their reasons, not mine, and they were entitled to decide for themselves why they were there, and what they would do once they were there. It did bring joy to my heart just knowing they were there, for whatever their reason!

Then, as I rounded one of the bends along the path, I came upon a little girl and her Mother. The little girl was probably 5 or 6 years old, and could not have been more adorable when she called out to her Mother; "Look Mommy, aren't the flowers beautiful? To which the Mother replied; "Oh my, they are very beautiful! Would you like to pick them and take them home?" The little girl smiled a smile that would warm the coldest heart, and answered; "No Mommy!"

The young Mother was shocked, it was obvious she (and I, being within hearing distance), thought for sure the little girl would've said "yes". She, the young Mother, and I were both anxious to hear why this little girl with a smile that would warm the coldest heart, so captivated by the beauty of the flowers before her, would choose "not to pick them" when clearly she was being given permission to do so. "Why don't you want to pick them?", asked the young Mother.

"Because if I pick them, they will die. If I leave them, they will live. I can see them again, and that will make me more happy!" And after saying that, the smile on her face and the warmth from her heart, would not have warmed only the coldest heart, but the entire Artic Ice Cap as well!

I will cherish the memory of that adorable little girl saying those simple and precious words; ". . . I can see them again, and that will make me more happy!" So firm was she in her FAITH, and in her BELIEF, that if she left them, if she let them grow, she would see them again in all their beauty! What a wonderful, wonderful, precious moment to witness, even more precious knowing that it was shared!

You see, the young Mother was giving her consent via question to pick the flowers that captivated her daughter's heart because she (the young Mother), knew they were "merely the flowers of weeds". So wonderful the example of "beauty being in the eye of the beholder", and of "the innocence and the purity of an untarnished heart"!

May WE all be reminded, by the memory of this child; "that if WE see that which is around US, if WE celebrate the Life, marvel at the brilliance, the magnificence of each thing, creature or person's uniqueness, be firm in OUR FAITH and BELIEF, allowing all to grow, and to go as they may need, WE will see them again on a beautiful day!"

May YOU and YOUR loved ones be blessed in all YOU do, may laughter and cheer warm your hearts through YOUR year. May sunshine and warmth be with YOU this day, and forever may YOU be ". . . more happy"!

21. TODAY I HEARD THE GRANDEST MUSIC OF ALL . . .

Today I heard the grandest music of all, the laughter of children straight from their hearts. So simple and pure, with no pretense, they were happy just being with family or friend sharing the moments until they would end. The giggling, the laughing, the whispering of forgotten jokes, poking and jabbing, tickling, tagging, holding hands, and making faces, not a cent did it cost but the memories priceless!

So fortunate are WE to bear witness to such joyful moments, even more fortunate when WE participate! But first WE must see, WE must become aware of that which is around US!

No matter how old or how young, whether home or abroad, no matter the profession, occupation, position or standing; WE have FREEDOM of CHOICE. WE can choose; to SEE, to slow down if necessary to become aware of that which is around US, and then WE can choose to bear witness, participate, share, experience, live!

Some may feel they are; all alone, too busy, too tired, too pressured, lost or confused, overworked, or worse too successful, too excited, too high in station or never left alone. Some may feel as if their Soul-mate or true friend will never be found or that hardship or abuse is their world without end!

WE have FREEDOM of CHOICE! WE can choose; to look within our mind and our heart to find our passion, our purpose, and pursue it. WE can choose to do so while being engaged, aware, and participating in the World around US.

When YOU choose to see, to slow down if necessary, to become aware of that which is around YOU, YOU will SEE as I and many others have chosen to SEE, WE are not alone nor will WE ever be; YOU will see the World with all its beauty and magnificence, You will come to realize; how fortunate YOU are when YOUR path crosses another's (and YOU will realize it was not by chance, but with purpose), and that if YOU allow YOURSELF to believe that, YOU will open the door and allow YOURSELF to see as YOU have never seen before, to feel as YOU have never felt before.

If at that moment, YOU BELIEVE in the ALMIGHTY, and ask for guidance, and have FAITH, the World as YOU had known it, will never be the same, the possibilities are infinitely better. Yes there are consequences to every decision made, so isn't it worth to; SEE more clearly, to be aware of the World around YOU, to know that which is within YOU, to believe in YOURSELF, in the ALMIGHTY, to have FAITH?

YES, it is!

YOU, me, WE are not alone nor will WE ever be! WE have FREEDOM of CHOICE! WE can choose; to SEE, to slow down if necessary to become aware of that which is around US, and then WE can choose to BELIEVE, to have FAITH, to LIVE OUR LIVES as they were meant to be lived, by participating! Today is THE DAY!

Today I choose hear the grandest music of all, the laughter of children! Care to listen?

Dare to be different, dare to be true, dare to be bold, DARE TO BE YOU! WE are all significant, each and every one of US! Shall WE begin?

22. WOULD YOU STAND TO DEFEND ANOTHER?

Would you stand to defend another? Would you run into a hail of bullets to save another? Would you battle evil for goodness sake?

Fortunate are WE to have Warriors that will stand in OUR defense every time duty calls! Fortunate are WE to have those that have chosen to serve and protect, uphold THE LAW, and seek JUSTICE where JUSTICE is due. Fortunate are WE to have those brave of heart, willing to battle raging fire to save others.

Fortunate are WE to have others BELIEVE in US, that have FAITH in US, that TRUST US to be there when WE are needed!

So I ask again; Would YOU stand to defend another? Would YOU run into a hail of bullets to save another? Would YOU battle evil for goodness sake? For there are moments in time, when YOU, when we as individuals, are the only ones there when circumstance asks the same question, and an answer MUST be given.

A hero by definition is; ". . . a mythological or legendary figure of great strength or ability, a man admired for his achievements and qualities, the chief male character in a literary or dramatic work . . ." (Webster dictionary), and heroine's definition would be similar with the exception of changing gender where necessary.

Each and every one of US has the ability to be heroic, for each and every one of US has the freedom of choice. When time or circumstance demands answers for such questions as asked above (or countless others), the choice is ours alone as an individual to make. Within each and every one of US, there are influences tugging at mind and heart, pushing and pulling US to decide one way or another, and all within a blink of eye.

In a classroom setting, you would hear countless argument or discussion about Nature or Nurture influencing OUR choices, about emotion (ah yes, love and hate can be powerful), about reasoning, about morals, about values, about beliefs. Bottom-line; when the crap hit's the fan, when a decision has to be made, will YOU stand or falter?

For me, I have found that when I have made peace within me before hand, when decision time comes, it is much easier for me to decide. By peace within me, I mean I have accepted and come to terms with what I value most and be willing to do, and what I value least and will never do.

My FAITH and my BELIEF in GOD, in LIFE everlasting, in that WE go on when OUR bodies fail US, is absolute, without question remaining, but that's me! My life's experiences based upon the consequences of decisions I have made, allowed me to arrive at where I am today.

You can too! I urge you, for your sake, and for the sake of all around you, especially those you so love and hold dear, that you look within your mind and heart, that you find that which you are passionate about, that you pursue it relentlessly, and by so doing, you discover your purpose! Have FAITH in that which you BELIEVE, dare to be different, dare to be true, dare to be bold, dare to be YOU!

Then live as you were meant to live, for life in this body of yours is finite (it will end, and very possibly without any advance warning). So LIVE, dare to be YOU! Have FAITH and BELIEVE, and you will find a peace within you that will allow you to answer those questions in a blink of an eye; Would you stand to defend another? Would you run into a hail of bullets to save another? Would you battle evil for goodness sake?

For me; Yes, I have and will always stand to defend another. Yes, I have run into a hail of bullets to save another, and will do so again without hesitation if need be. Yes, I have battled evil for goodness sake, and I always, always will!

And if these were to be the last words I'd say, these words I'd leave you for each day; "I believe in you, I believe in me, I believe in WE! Have FAITH, BELIEVE, for WE are not alone nor will WE ever be. BELIEVE!"

May WE all be reminded by the senseless and tragic act of violence in Aurora, Colorado that took the lives of 12, and injured 59 in body, and thousands (if not millions more) within mind and heart, that life here is finite, and LIFE with FAITH and BELIEF in GOD is everlasting! May all reach out to those in their hours of need with OUR thoughts and prayers. May all find Peace! Shall WE begin?

23. WE ARE NOT ALONE

In the World in which WE live, there seems to be a spiritual disconnect on a grander scale by the day. Many, seem to have lost their way, and have forgotten how to ask for help.

Simply believe in GOD, have faith, and when faced with a difficult path or decision, just ask yourself this question; What would Jesus do or say (WWJD)?

By taking the time to ask yourself that question, things have a way of becoming much clearer and easier to understand, options seem to appear, solutions seem to be much more logical, and you feel good inside.

WE are not alone, believe, have faith, ask yourself the question; "What would Jesus do?" Answer it, then do what you feel in your heart to be right. You'll be amazed at the results!

Now is the time, believe, have faith, get busy. Today is the first day of the rest of your life!

24. HIS HAND IS REACHING FOR YOURS, IT'S TIME YOU TOOK IT!

Today, March 29th, 2013 is "GOOD FRIDAY", and as is the case on many a morning commute, a child's question to her Mother caught my ear; "Mommy, if today is the day God's Son died, why is it good? Wasn't HE sad? Didn't his Mommy cry? Shouldn't it be Bad Friday or Sad Friday?

I love the simplicity and the directness of children, they are hungry to learn, and simply want answers!

In reality, depending upon which YOU have been taught or have heard, in early English and Dutch, Good was thought to mean Holy, and so the perspective would be one more of "God's Friday". Either way, over the expanse of time, it is now most commonly known as "Good Friday".

So let's gain some perspective here, is this a day of celebration or sadness, a day of significance or hype?

First off, straight out, I must confess I am absolutely, positively, 100% convinced and believe without any question that Jesus walked this Earth, that Jesus was born from Mary, that God is His Father from Heaven above, and so, I am biased because of these beliefs.

That said, let's continue to get more perspective, and answers. Many people of varying beliefs, of varying religions seldom take the time or interest to learn about other beliefs, and religions. I am not one of them, for I love to learn, especially about people's history, and religions are a HUGE and important factor in all peoples' history.

Did you know, that nearly every single religion acknowledges Jesus did exist, that He was a prophet, if not the Son of God as Christians believe, that He was born from Mary, that He was imprisoned, tortured, ridiculed, nailed to a cross and left to die, that while he walked the Earth, He healed those in need, spoke of His Father, and that which was to come (to include His death, and that He would rise again).

More perspective, from another set of eyes, that of His Mother, Mary; seeing her son having been bruised, beaten, flesh torn with thorns, splinters from carrying His cross (and the burden of that which He chose to carry on OUR behalf), spikes driven through His limbs nailing Him to the cross (oh how the sound of each blow of the hammer as it struck the spike deeper through her son's flesh and bone, the screams of agony and pain of her son), seeing Him (her son, the Son of GOD in Heaven) nailed to that cross and left to die a slow excruciating death. And hearing His words to His Heavenly Father as death approached; ". . . Father, forgive them, for they know not what they do . . ." Luke 34, can YOU imagine the pain in MARY'S heart (near insane must she have been at that moment realizing death was now knocking)! Darkness descended, and the light of Mankind was lit for eternity!

Now picture a Father with but one son, know that Father to be God in Heaven above, His Son given ever so freely with nothing but love for the benefit of all Mankind, to free them of sin, to give them another chance to do right, to do good, to love and serve each other, to cherish LIFE for what it was and is, a gift from HIM to all of Mankind for eternity, and this is what man does? Do YOU see THAT FATHER near insane with anger, nearing the point when vengeance was not a thought, but GOD'S Will? Then, HE hears HIS SON'S words; ". . . Father, forgive them, for they know not what they do . . ." Luke 34, and then the greatest story ever told has "come to be reality", GOD'S covenant fulfilled; Christ the SON had been born, HE lived, and HE died, so that all Mankind's sins would be forgiven, so that all people could repent and have the HOPE of everlasting LIFE if they (WE) choose to BELIEVE!

I have been to the Mountain Top, bathed in the BRILLIANCE of HIS GLORY, and KNOW, WE are NOT alone nor will WE ever be, DARE TO BE YOU! Now is the time, TODAY is THE DAY! BELIEVE! Shall WE begin?

25. ONE OF GOD'S GREATEST BLESSINGS IS LIFE

One of God's greatest of all blessings is LIFE, and with it, opportunity to be that which we are capable of being, to do that which we are capable of doing, to find our passion and pursue it, and the choice is ultimately ours to make, and no others!

And along our way, we are further blessed with guardians in one form or another; a parent, a sibling, a teacher, a friend, a neighbor, an angel, HIS HAND.

The joy of a parent seeing their child, watching them grow, sharing the triumphs and tragedies, the hits and the misses, the successes and the failures while the child travels their journey, is without equal, and a blessing of such magnificence in its own right, and yet there IS even more to LIFE! How could anyone possibly think mankind is NOT blessed!

My son Michael will be 25 in mere days, and of him (as I am of his step-brother Joseph, and his sister Anna Lynn), I could not be more proud nor more blessed for having had the privilege and the honor to have been so fortunate to have shared in their journey thus far, and to see how wonderful they have become!

But, we all know, that every journey has its perils, its ups and downs, and all arounds, and so choices must be made, and every choice has a consequence.

Consequence, seldom is the word given as much thought before a decision is made, as it's given after (provided there is the ability to think, and one is alive). Hell, if every single person was to provide the consequences of every decision being made endlessly, nothing would ever get accomplished, and every person would be stuck as if in concrete as they attempted to travel their journey. And so, through education, through "experience" learned from consequences of previous choices, we grow, we get better, and gain the ability and the confidence to make even better and more timely choices at critical moments in the future.

Such experiences that helped to teach us that which can be done better, more timely, more efficiently, can often become the true difference between living and dying when choices have to be made at a brake neck speed later, especially if your journey is one of a policeman, fireman, serviceman, health professional, etc.

So, I for one, throughout my military life, and life thereafter, often found, and still find myself drawn to those that have made choices, lived and learned from the consequences of their decisions, for they have gotten even better then they were (and let's face reality, if you were a professional in a hazardous job, and one of your peers learned what could be a life saving lesson that very well could save many lives at another time, to include yours, wouldn't YOU want to be partnered with that person at the first, and every, opportunity in the future? I WOULD, and DID every time I could, and maybe that's why I'm still here).

You see, seldom if ever, will you make the same choice if the consequence of the first choice turned bad, and you allowed yourself to learn from it. There is GOOD to be learned when things go bad. There is success after failure when you get up, and choose NOT TO FAIL, for sometimes, sometimes; "FAILURE IS NOT AN OPTION".

Like the Phoenix, we can rise to unprecedented heights of our choosing when we learn our lessons well, teach others what we have learned, our journey grows grander, our blessings multiplied, and OUR World is the better for it!

And so to my son Michael, and to all those in Blue of whom know me I say; there is no other I'd rather have at my side then you, Michael, when WE are to knock at HELL'S door! Semper Fidelis!

26. BEAUTY ONLY SKIN DEEP?
WHAT SAY YOU?

Is beauty only skin deep, as it has been said or as we have been told? Is beauty in the eye of the beholder, would that mean the blind cannot see beauty? What say you? Have you seen beauty for beauty's sake? Is beauty only seen or is it experienced? Is beauty reliant upon mutual emotion, thought, stimulus, perspective?

I have been dumb-struck, rendered speechless by the beauty of a newborn child, for there before me I saw the miracle of life anew, reassuring all of US that God still had HOPE for mankind with seemingly infinite possibility of that which could be, of that which would be!

Is not the laughter of a child while rubbing noses with a parent, family or friend while each others cheeks are held in loving outstretched hands face to face, a site of beauty to behold and cherish?

I have seen many a bruised, battered, broken, seemingly lifeless body amidst mounds of death and destruction, that hearing or feeling my footsteps, have turned and smiled washing away their pain and despair. Could not such a moment be more beautiful! I'm telling you, it could not!

I have been blessed with many a friend that have a gift, a talent to see that which is, from a perspective not seen by many, and they capture in in photo or word, and share that which is for all the World to see.

Aren't the experiences, the wisdom, the knowledge, the emotions gained, shared, realized through life's journey critical pieces to a simply magnificent mosaic of each and all of us, that when situations in our lives afford us the opportunity to finally see, experience, and appreciate, beautiful?

Is not a Mother, a sister, a daughter that has advanced in years sacrificing any or everything, enduring discomfort or sorrow along with moments of joy more beautiful than near anything or anyone else when fully realized? Yes she, they are!

And so I ask again; "Is beauty only skin deep? Can those without sight know beauty?

Beauty is not only skin deep, for at times, skin is of little significance to the beauty that abounds within! Beauty is to be experienced!

May WE all be fortunate enough to experience Beauty for Beauty sake, to share such Beauty for all the World to see, and to marvel at how simple it can truly be. Experience that which is around US, sing praise, and be thankful! Shall WE begin?

27. HOW WOULD "YOU" FEEL IF . . .

You hear a cry for help; "Please somebody help me, help me
please! Please, somebody HELP ME! SOMEBODY, PLEASE
HELP ME!! Do you not hear? HELP MEEEEEEEEEEEEE,
PLEASEEEEEEEEEE!!"

Through the darkness you travel, with all the speed of foot,
pushing, pulling, clawing and tearing, lifting and bearing crushed
concrete and dust. With THUNDEROUS ROAR you let out your
voice; "I'M COMING YOU HEAR! HOLD ON I'M NEAR!
HOLD ON, DO YOU HEAR!!!!!!!!!!!!!!!! (Command, not question).

No answer is given, not a sound do you hear, not a wimpy, a cry
nor drop of a tear!

You THUNDER your words as you SMASH through the wall;
"HOLD ON, I'M HERE! HOLD ON, DO YOU HEAR!!!!!!!!!!!!!!!

No Life is before you, no movement, no sound; you fall to your
knees with your head way back, SCREAMING to HEAVEN;
"HELP ME DEAR LORD, PLEASE HELP ME THIS DAY,
DON'T TAKE HIM DEAR LORD, THIS I DO PRAY!"

There's a flame burning within your heart that you feel, a
voice calling in the depths of your ear; "I'M COMING YOU
HEAR, HOLD ON I'M NEAR! HOLD ON, DO YOU HEAR?
(QUESTION)

With FAITH and BELIEF you answer; "I DO!" You work like
lightning, doing all that you know, never doubting for a second of
that which will show, LIFE!

More help does arrive, and out you all go, to the land of the living, while thanking "HE" for the show!

How would "YOU" feel if: You hear a cry for help; "Please somebody help me, help me please! PLEASE, somebody HELP ME!! SOMEBODY, PLEASE HELP ME!! Do you not hear? HELP MEEEEEE, PLEASEEEEEE!!", and you're standing on a crowded train platform, walking in a Mall, bathing at the beach, dropping your child off at school, vacationing in a park, watching a ballgame from your reserved seats?

HOW WOULD "YOU" FEEL IF "YOU" WERE THE ONE CALLING, AND "NO ONE" ANSWERED?

HAVE FAITH, BELIEVE, WE are not alone nor will WE ever be! BELIEVE!

Remember these words in all that you do; "I'M COMING YOU HEAR, HOLD ON I'M NEAR! HOLD ON, DO YOU HEAR?" (Question) For such will be GOD'S answer every time you call. And with your FAITH and BELIEF then answer; "I DO!"

28. IT'S NEVER TOO LATE!

You're cruising along, young or old it matters not, you're feeling good, your life and circumstance are going your way! Life just doesn't get any better! It's a beautiful day! Then, BAM!!!!

Whether accident, injury, Nature, man-made, whether illness or heartache, games people played, financial ruin or economy collapse, family lost or family astray, it's never too late!

For whatever the reason, it is what it is; depending on how you were raised you believe what you want, you feel the way you want, you act the way you want, you think the way you want, you respond the way you want.

"My World has been shattered", "my dreams are a bust", "the injury too great", "my love now lust", "my pockets were full and now thread bare", "what the hell will I do from the depths of my despair?"

Tired and broken, sick you may be, hungry, cold, with thirst of three, or penniless with your clothes in a tatter, you feel lost and alone and nothing does matter! It's never too late!

There's a reason for being, YOU are HERE THIS DAY, lift your head to the LORD, and begin to pray;

"I'm here before you for reasons I know not, I hear a distant calling from within my heart, to lift my head to Heaven and ask you this day; to help me dear Lord, this I do pray!"

Be firm in your FAITH, believe in your heart, trust in the Lord, and simply just start. It's never too late!

Do what you can, think of a plan, dare to be different, dare to be true, dare to be bold, dare to be YOU! It's never too late! One step at a time is all you need take, fear not, and believe, "It's never too late!"

With FAITH did I pray, with BELIEF in my heart, I trusted Our Lord, got busy, got started. One step did I take, one step at a time, progress was made not costing a dime. It's never too late!

I searched the World over, and found this to be true; I was firm in my FAITH, and BELIEF in my heart, "I DARED TO BE ME", and got a new start! IT'S NEVER TOO LATE! Believe!

29. HEAR THE MUSIC, FEEL THE BEAT . . . CHOOSE TO DANCE!

I love music, especially Latino music, but all music empowers me, for it frees me; to think, to feel, to see, to create, to experience, to share, to cherish all Life has to offer, and that which I can offer others.

I love the passion in Latino music, in seconds your body simply wants to move, to twist, to turn, to reach, to bend, to leap, to soar, to spin. But, best of all, you want to do all that with another at your side, in a beautiful and majestic harmony of pose, balance, purpose, and design of two as one! It's magic!

I met my wife at work, but I fell in love with her on the dance floor at our company Holiday party in 1986. The music played, my hand touched hers and I was gone, forever hers; we moved as if one, hours seemed like minutes, everything just fit perfectly, seldom did our feet stop, our hearts never missing a beat. The party ended, we left as we came, in separate cars, but already our hearts were one, for the music was there!

Twenty-eight years later, we're still together, and I still feel the music within my heart!

In all that I do, in all that I see, in all that I experience during my day, there's music to the madness, a rhythm to life. Many get so caught up in what they are doing, in what has to be done, in deadlines (and I'm sure, rightfully so), that often the music, the rhythm to their life goes by without notice, and they miss an opportunity to strengthen their purpose, their passion for Life, their Life!

For I believe each and every one of us is unique, is significant, and does have a purpose, a reason for being, and when we look within our minds, and our hearts, when we find our passion, our purpose, and pursue it relentlessly, WE as individuals, and WE as a People, benefit greatly, and make Life's music even grander!

Have you ever seen a Master Craftsman / Tradesman at what WE assume would be work, to him or her it's love and opportunity to create something to the best of their ability, willfully! I've witnessed many such Craftsman with Iron, Steel, Wood, Brick, Tile, Paint, Earth, Water, and I marvel at their brilliance, their discipline, their utter delight at that which they are doing!

Have you seen and heard a Musician so talented that you honestly felt as if GOD put them here specifically for the delight of all HIS children? I have, often!

Have you ever seen or experienced the drive and determination of many Professionals in Fire, in Rescue, in Law Enforcement, in the Military, who willfully greet chaos daily for the benefit of others, and from within their depths, you see them find their rhythm and overcome all obstacles for the sole purpose of doing that which they believe to be right, and necessary to help or to protect another? I have! It's awesome!

Have you ever seen or experienced the love of a Parent for their child? The music that plays from their heart through their words, their actions, their sacrifices, is deafening, and brings tears of great joy, willfully!

All around US, Man and Nature perform their greatest symphony when in harmony, for their music calls to OUR very Souls, igniting the passion within US all, stimulating thought and creativity to even greater heights, and all OUR World benefits!

So this I ask of all of YOU; Hear the Music within YOU, and around YOU, feel the beat, get on YOUR feet, and choose to DANCE! Now is OUR time, shall WE begin?

30. THANKSGIVING, WHAT A WONDERFUL HOLIDAY!

One of the greatest holidays of the whole year is "Thanksgiving Day"! Why? Because every race, religion, culture, people of any and all ages, can find something and / or someone to be thankful for. So, every single one of US can participate!

Rather than list what I am thankful for, I ask each and all of you to take a few moments to think about your own lives, no matter pain, heartache, discomfort, in convenience you may have encountered, I'm sure that when you step back and look through eyes willing to see, you'll glimpse something that warmed your heart, made you laugh, made you love, eased your pain, gave you hope, inspired you to try again. While you're looking, maybe, you'll be surprised by all that has gone right amidst that which has gone wrong (you just didn't realize it at that moment).

You'll see, as have I, that WE have much to be thankful for (things could always be worse). So, let US all celebrate that which each of US can be thankful for. Even if only for a few minutes in privacy, give thanks, and if you really want to enrich your heart, and experience great joy on this day of Thanksgiving, do a Random Act of Kindness for Family, for friend, for someone you never met before! It's wonderful, and the warmth you will experience within your heart and soul will be long remembered.

Many Peoples around the globe now partake in this wonderful and simple holiday! Can you imagine how many Random Acts of Kindness could be accomplished on this of all days! Would not the shear number of people that could benefit warm all OUR hearts? What a wonderful holiday!

You, me, WE, boy could WE do a lot of good in one day, and each in simple and affordable ways! I urge you to participate; first by taking a step back and looking through fresh eyes, look to see that which you are thankful for, and second, by doing a Random Act of Kindness. Try it, what do you have to lose?

Have a Happy Thanksgiving!

I believe in YOU, I believe in ME, I believe in WE, and WE CAN DO BETTER with each Random Act of Kindness we'll see! Shall WE begin?

31. FOR OUR CHILDREN, AND THAT WHICH CAN BE . . .

In near all places around this World, of which WE are a part, babies are born. Customs and cultures may differ, but more often than not, the wish of their parent(s), for their baby, is Life, love, and that which can and should be; long and healthy life with friend and family.

Many a parent have I met, in lands far and near, in peace, in war, on sea or shore, and seldom have I heard that wish vary.

So, the love for OUR children, the wish for the love of OUR children, and their long life, is a common thread that unites US, excites US, and gives ample cause for celebration as each baby advances another year.

Well, on this eve of Christmas, this day before many of US celebrate the birth of Jesus as OUR Savior, it is fitting to note that near every race, religion, culture, acknowledges His existence, and those not proclaiming Him to be the Son of God, do call Him Prophet, and have documented many of His good works, miracles, teachings. The point, HE lived; HE was born, a baby, a child, a teen, then a man. HE was a son with parents who loved Him, as much as any parent should.

Recently, here in the USA, many lives were lost in a tragic act of violence, many children along with some adults, innocent were they all, but death found them, and took them!

The World over, babies die each and every day, some young, some old, but somebody's baby nevertheless.

So OUR World is no stranger to loss nor to the extreme pain, torment, heartache and sorrow that accomplishes each and every one! For WE mourn the loss of each child!

Picture now the pain, the anguish, the heartache of God when HIS Son was betrayed, tortured, humiliated, spit upon, and left to die nailed upon a cross! With anger and hurt swelling to near breaking point, HE hears the words of HIS Son pleading to HIM on OUR behalf; ". . . Forgive them Father, for they know not what they do . . ." Luke 34, and upon hearing that, HIS FATHER, GOD forgives MAN, for such is HIS greatness, such is HIS love for US as well!

And with the birth of each baby, HE reminds US all; that HE still has HOPE for US to chooses more wisely, to BELIEVE, and to have FAITH in HIM. If HE has not given upon US, how dare We give up on HIM!

So this Christmas eve, this Christmas Day, let US all remember what WE are truly celebrating; the birth of OUR SAVIOR, by whom WE were granted the opportunity to live LIFE as it was meant to be lived; by choosing good over evil, right over wrong, to help over hurt.

Let US show HIM that WE BELIEVE, WE have FAITH, and that WE choose to make a difference, for WE know WE can, and We must do better! Shall WE begin?

32. IT'S A NEW DAY! YOUR TIME HAS COME!

As 2012 draws to a close, many of us will think back upon the year and wonder where the time went! We'll find ourselves asking; "Can another year really be over, already?"

For some, the year could not have ended soon enough for a variety of reasons! Tragic events such as; death and destruction from storms and floods, death and /or incapacitating injury from illness, accident, war, senseless act of violence, devastated many of us, our families, our communities, our cities, states, Nation!

Even while thousands, and thousands of people, of families were reeling and trying to cope with "Life after Hurricane Sandy" (thinking life could not possibly get worse), the senseless shooting of children an their teachers smacked US all right across the face, and broke many a mending heart beyond repair. "HOW COULD THIS BE HAPPENING?"

"What the HELL is going on?" If I am dreaming; PLEASE WAKE ME UP!"

But it was no dream, and it continued; a 4-year old little girl found dead in a vacant bone chilling parking lot, commuters minding their own business pushed in front of subway trains, killing them, on and on!

Each and all of US are no strangers to stories / incidents such as these, not this year, especially since information now flows the World over in mere seconds! But, in fact, "that information now flows the World over in mere seconds" can also be a blessing if WE so choose!

PROCRASTINATION, putting off until later that which could be done now, robs us all of treasures that are priceless! Its consequences can destroy lives, families, communities, towns, states, Nations, and damn our very Souls to Hell (if we so choose).

No one makes us procrastinate except, ourselves! No one! No matter what BS YOU come up with in YOUR own defense, NO ONE makes us procrastinate except us, OURSELVES! The choice is made by us alone, and most frequently because it is the path of least resistance, least effort, least conflict. No wonder it's choice proves to cause heartache and sorrow every time!

So DO SOMETHING ABOUT IT, make YOUR LIFE BETTER RIGHT NOW, THIS INSTANT! Make a decision to NOT PROCRASTINATE starting right now. The choice is YOURS to make, make it, don't procrastinate and make YOUR decision "LATER"!

Feel the POWER in these words; "I WILL NOT PROCRASTINATE, I WILL DO IT NOW!"

A quote that my Father use to repeat to me often is so appropriate and inspiring, unfortunately I do not know the original author and I do not claim it to be from my Father or I. I do want to share it with YOU because of the truth to it;

". . . We shall pass this way but once, All the good that can be done; do it now, For WE shall not pass this way again." author unknown to me

Now as your days and nights progress, as you are faced with decisions to make, you can overcome your fears, your worries, for you will say to yourself; "I WILL NOT PROCRASTINATE, I WILL DO IT NOW; whatever I MUST to allow myself to arrive at the point where my decision can be made." You decide, you act, you deal with consequence, you move on!

You hug a little longer, laugh a little louder, reach out sooner, say what needs to be said, open your heart, enrich your Soul, do what you must, discover your passion, pursue it relentlessly for as long as it takes, learn to listen, hear what's said, discover the World around you, bury your dead!

Let kindness, warmth, caring, sharing, love, and laughter fill your heart, enrich your mind, strengthen your Soul. Have FAITH, and BELIEF in GOD above. Dream of that which could some day be, have HOPE, and pray to be shown the way!

Dare to be different, dare to be true, dare to be bold, DARE TO BE YOU! Know in YOUR mind, know in YOUR heart, YOU are significant, and TODAY IS YOUR FRESH START! A new day has dawned!

YOU make a difference; One act of Kindness per day, one kind word well timed, an outstretched hand to welcome another, the choice is YOURS to make!

Shall WE begin?

33. CAN "YOU" CHANGE YOUR WORLD

Does not a baby learn to walk with but the first step, ONE step, then another? Does not a baby learn to speak with but the first word, ONE word, then another? Does not any journey, grand or small, begin with but the first step, ONE step, then another?

Whether you are young or old, well kept or unclean, educated or of simple mind, you, and you alone as ONE, can change your World! The reality is, that with each decision, each choice made by you, there is consequence (be it good or ill), and YOUR World has been changed. The power to create, to shape, to mold YOUR WORLD is within you, in your thoughts, and every decision you make will have consequence, defining what your World will be. So, are your thoughts worthy of your time?

Is your World in which you are in at this moment, how you want it to be? THINK! Picture in your mind the World in which YOU would like to live; search your mind and your heart and find your passion. Think and FEEL that which is within you, and see yourself as only YOU can. Now BELIEVE, in mind, in heart, in Soul, that which will be, have FAITH! Think of a plan to get you where you want to be, think of the first step, decide to take it, ONE step, and then another. Are you not changing YOUR World?

If YOU are firm in FAITH, implementing your plan, traveling your journey, progressing towards that which you believe will be, and I see from where you've come, can I not be inspired? Will not your FAITH, your BELIEF, your decision to travel your journey be not of a positive influence on me, and inspire me; to THINK, to FEEL that which is within me, to BELIEVE in my mind, heart, and Soul that which will be. FAITH will I have, decision will I make, first step taken, then another. Will not the World in which I live be changed?

If your World has been changed, and my World has been changed, has not the World in which WE both live been changed?

If along our journeys, we positively influence others in word, in thought, in action, have WE not changed our World?

So I ask you; "Can YOU change YOUR World? Can WE change OUR World?

Do YOU BELIEVE? Do YOU have FAITH?

Dare to be different, dare to be true, dare to be bold, dare to be YOU! I believe in you, I believe in me, I believe in WE! Shall WE begin?

34. "WRITE WHAT YOU KNOW, THE GREATEST, AND . . .

"Write what you know", the greatest, and yet the hardest lesson for those with a love for writing to learn, understand, and accept! Why?

Ah, there's the most dreaded question of every parent from their child; "Why?" (dreaded mainly because as soon as you answer the very first time, the child knows you are listening, and wants to learn about that which he has a question, and since the child is in his youth, and the World is before him, the question flood-gate "Why?", can at times, appear endless, and truly test the patience of even the most loving and seasoned parent / teacher).

Quite simply; When a writer writes what they know, the writer has an opportunity to share that which is known more successfully, and in that regard, the writer is similar to everyone else that "knows something" and wishes to influence others in the World in which WE all live.

So, and a big "so" I might add, since I love to write, what do I know that I can write about that can be of interest to YOU, that would be worthy of YOUR time?

And what I know is this; "YOU were born, YOU live, and the day will come when YOU will die, BUT, after YOU die, there is LIFE, and those so well loved will be seen by YOU again. I know YOU are significant, YOU have a purpose, a reason for being, and only YOU with FAITH and BELIEF in God, with HIS Loving Hand and assistance through a variety of means and circumstance will discover that purpose when YOU look within YOUR mind, and YOUR heart. I know when YOU pursue that which is within YOU, passionately, relentlessly, firm in YOUR FAITH and BELIEF, OUR

78

World will be all the better for it! I know YOU are significant! YOUR time is now, for YOU are here NOW!

The choice is YOURS to make! Are YOU not worthy of YOUR time? Is not FAITH and BELIEF in God worthy of YOUR time and effort when it is HE who granted YOU Life, and who, when asked, will help YOU?

Have not YOU noticed that things have become more difficult at home, within OUR communities, cities, States, Nations, the World over? Have YOU not noticed the subtle changes in OUR societies, the straying of believing in good conquering evil, of doing what's right over what's wrong, of people actually feeling embarrassed to say they BELIEVE in God and Heaven?

Do not OUR children see this? And WE have the nerve to challenge and question God when things go terribly wrong by the choices WE have made?

Heaven is for real! God is for real! WE are here because it is HIS WILL, and no other reason, and WE sure as HELL better embrace that thought and belief. No sooner will the tide turn in OUR favor, then when WE choose to make it so!

With the birth of every child, God shows US all that HE has not given up on US, that HE has HOPE for US, that HE believes in US, and that which WE are capable of, and WE are capable of DOING BETTER, NOW!

As a Parent, is it not OUR wish to see OUR children live? Is it not OUR desire, OUR HOPE, to see OUR children do better, in a World that is BETTER? And whose example is it they are to follow?

WE are the children of God; and no matter what OUR age (young or old), that child lives within US. Many will ask, have asked themselves and others how WE (they), could believe in God when such terrible and tragic things happen (especially when things happen to children).

I ask; HOW COULD WE NOT BELIEVE IN GOD? With the loss of even one child, WE are devastated, often appearing and acting grief stricken beyond any possible recovery (and at those moments, under those circumstances, appearing rightly so). But now try to imagine God looking down upon Earth, and what happens to millions of HIS children daily, and yet HE believes still in US, and grants the birth of another (but for how long will HE tolerate OUR choices). WE MUST DO BETTER!

Are YOU, ARE OUR CHILDREN, ARE WE not worthy of OUR effort, OUR choice to do, and to be better? Of course WE are! What can be done? Where do WE start? There is only one place, and each of US must do it ourselves, and God will help US if we ask!

But first WE must have FAITH and BELIEF, we must awaken that which is within US; As OUR newborns reach out to US with loving outstretched hands, longing for OUR unconditional loving embrace, reach out to GOD as many times as YOU must, for YOUR prayers will be heard!

There is a wonderful, wonderful book that has been released in a child's illustrated version, and I urge YOU all to get it or at least to put it in YOUR own hands, and for YOU to read and view from front to back, again, I'm referring to a specific version, for a specific reason, YOUR heart and YOUR Soul will understand when YOU are done.

It is; "Heaven is for Real for Kids", as told by Colton Burpo to his Parents Todd & Sonja Burpo, ILLUSTRATED by Wilson Ong.

There is no better book to ease any Parent, Family, Friends aching heart resulting from recent events, than this one, especially for children!

I have no affiliation with anyone associated with this book except for my FAITH and BELIEF in GOD above, and my intent in urging YOU to put it in YOUR hands, and for YOU to read it, and view it, is solely to benefit YOU, and YOUR loved ones! By so doing, I hope, trust, and pray better and more timely choices will be made, and ultimately as a result, YOU will come to realize as I do; WE WILL DO BETTER for the CHOICE is OURS to make, and WE, OUR children, OUR World, are worthy of OUR time and effort for WE are here NOW!

Shall WE begin?

35. YOUR EYES ARE OPEN, MAY YOU NOW SEE!

Being at the Ronkonkoma Train Station each morning at 3:40 am is an experience on normal days. Being there on the platform awaiting the arrival of the 4:06 am train to Penn Station on bad weather days is an adventure!

On one particularly frigid morning, with the wind whipping through the platforms, many of the regulars were absent, and one young lady that was normally surrounded by a group of Tradesmen, found herself standing alone in her normal spot. Unknown to me, she had already made her decision to move over to where I was waiting so that she would no longer be standing alone.

Since she was blind, when she arrived next to me, I thought maybe she had become disoriented because many of the regulars were not where they normally would have been, so I mentioned to her that she was now standing one train car distance past her normal spot. She told me she knew, and had decided to move over to where she knew I would be standing so that she would not be standing alone. I told her I would be happy to keep her company.

Shortly thereafter, the train arrived, we boarded and took seats near one another. She told me she had to be at work in the city at 9am, and had found that taking the early train helped her navigate the city better because with smaller crowds and less traffic, she could hear, smell, and feel landmarks with greater ease. I was amazed, but not surprised at how she adapted to her circumstance out of necessity (for in all my years, and travels, I had seen many people that had made the most out of adversity, affliction, or circumstance that was anything other than favorable).

WE ended our conversation as the train departed the station, both happy knowing someone was nearby as we traveled to Penn (at that hour, nearly everyone drifts off to sleep as soon as the train pulls out of the station, knowing that they could sleep for at least an hour before they have to start listening to announcements).

We arrived at Penn, and went our separate ways.

Some days have now passed, and this morning, the atmosphere at Penn Station was different, dangerous different, especially at our usual 5:15am arrival time. The night had again been bitterly cold, with a bone chilling wind, so the number of homeless in Penn was larger, as was the number of troublemakers (most of the homeless, don't want trouble, don't make trouble, they just want to be warm, eat something, and be left alone). In the wee hours, a criminal element does make itself visible, even in Penn, watching, waiting for opportunity, and if YOU GIVE IT TO THEM, believe YOU me, THEY POUNCE. The Law Enforcement Officers respond (for they are there too), but the damage is already done.

So, on this morning, when the air at Penn seemed hostile, I could not take my mind off worrying about the dangers the handicapped have to face daily, the homeless have to face daily, especially (as in the young lady's case that shared the platform with me days before), if they are blind, and yet, they do, seldom with complaint! I could not help but to say a prayer, asking God to protect that young lady, and all that are in need of HIS assistance.

So many of US are blessed with so much more than WE are fully aware, I urge YOU to allow yourself the opportunity daily, to reflect upon YOUR many blessings, and to give thanks to God for that which YOU do have. I ask that YOU allow yourself to become aware of those of whom may be in need of assistance around YOU, and if possible, do that which YOU can!

I believe in YOU, I believe in ME, I believe in WE, and WE make a difference one way or another. May WE hear that which calls from within OUR heart, choose to listen, and to get involved, for OUR World is all the better for it! Shall WE begin?

36. SOMETIMES, THE SIMPLEST PLEASURES CAN BRING GREAT JOY

Sometimes, the simplest of pleasures can bring great joy, and just make any hardship so much more tolerable!

When I first got my train this morning (at 3:55am), I placed my backpack down on the seat next to me so that it was easier to find an item I was looking for, take it out, and put to use. One of the young tradesmen that sits near me watched what I was doing, and could not help but to make a comment when he saw what I pulled out, and immediately put to use; "Hey, old timer, aren't you supposed to use those things when you're outside, you know, in the cold" (keep in mind we were presently sitting inside the train that was about to depart westbound to Penn Station, NYC).

What "those things" are (that he was referring to, that I had pulled out, and had put to use), are "HOT HANDS Hand Warmers". They come as a pair, individually wrapped, ready to use, air activated, safe, and provide natural heat / warmth lasting 4-6 hours. Quite simply; they are magnificent!

You see, in some ways, the years, and my adventures have taken a toll on parts of me, my hands definitely; they have been broken, smashed, cut, and subjected to damn near every temp and environment imaginable. I have scar tissue in half my fingers, and my right thumb looks so disfigured from having been smashed and healing in a different position (as compared to my left thumb), that YOU could think another person's right thumb was attached to replace mine (it wasn't).

Anyone with damaged hands (healed broken bones, scar tissue), would certainly tell you that they are no fun when they get cold in near freezing temps! The best way to describe hands and fingers with scar tissue in the cold, is simply to have YOU picture ice cubes under YOUR skin with no way to remove them, and as the day goes on, the cold just seems to intensify and spread to the good parts as well. Quite frankly, it stinks, and makes for an extremely long day / night!

Well, 80% of my 10 hour workday is outside or in unheated work spaces, and add commuting / platform time to that, and conservatively it averages to about 14 hours (sometimes longer) each day.

So when winter approached this year 2012 /2013, I dreaded the cold to come. I made up my mind to find relief other than super insulted gloves (my work requires me to remove my gloves frequently, sometimes for long periods of time). HOT HANDS Hand Warmers provided wonderful relief, and when my wife, Diane, heard about how much they helped, she surprised me with a HUGE supply of them!

I have found that if I combine the HOT HANDS with dollar store fleece gloves, the warmth provided to my hands is amazing, and almost instantly rids my hands of that ice cube sensation, so my day is so much more tolerable than it had been previously.

So pleasurable has it become, that like this morning with the temp slightly above freezing, I was anxious to expose the HOT HANDS to the air (air activated), insert them into my dollar store fleece gloves while on my morning commute, and sleep away for an hour and 10 minutes in hand warmth heaven!

Of course I provided the inquiring young tradesman with a shortened version, but he understood, and was satisfied with the answer.

After we arrived at Penn Station, and went our separate ways, I continued on, walking North on 7th Ave to 34th street, then 34th over to 6th Ave to catch the F subway uptown and get off a few blocks from work, and walk the rest of the way.

As I walked, I was SO happy with the warmth in my hands, and the warmth in my heart (because my wife, Diane, bought so many of them for me that I knew my hands will not be cold as ice again unless I put them in our freezer on purpose, and I won't).

Such a simple pleasure, and what great joy does it bring! What a nice way to start the day, I almost wish it wasn't Friday night so I could do it again in a few hours (what a line, just kidding. Friday nights are my most favorite time of all to be home because my weekend has just begun and is at its longest).

Well, I hope your hands are warm, and YOUR heart is as well, and may YOU too indulge in life's simple pleasures and possibly, share one or two with those in need as well! May joy and warmth fill your heart! Shall WE begin?

37. LEARN THE GOOD WHEN THINGS GO BAD

When we are young, and as we progress through our youthful years, we learn, we experience, thoughts, dreams, desires get our attention, and often we act or react to life's events or situations failing to realize that others (like parents, family, friends) may have very well had extremely similar events happen in their lives. So, when they offer a story, a comment, a suggestion with the hope or intent to help or to prevent you (us) from experiencing discomfort, pain, sorrow, we don't truly listen / hear that which is said; for there is more to words than letters, there's love, there's prayer, there's promise, there's tomorrow, there's HOPE, there's wisdom!

Yes, no two people honestly can ever feel or be the same, for we are different. But we can be extremely similar, and very darn close at times, especially in moments when things go terribly wrong or wonderfully right! Human nature remains the same and emotions have that way of bringing out the worst or the best in us.

But to you, the young in age, in heart, in mind, and body, know this; your parents, family, friends believe in you, have faith in you, and want all to be well with you, will stand by you, and understand you will travel YOUR path!

Dare YOU not respect or dare YOU make little the path they have had or chosen to travel, the sacrifices they have made, and continue to make willfully, lovingly, to allow you to get where you are this day, and to be available to you should you need or want their assistance. For YOU are the World to them!

So, as you travel your path, the path you have chosen, as you experience your life's many events (great and small), gain perspective, learn to see, allow yourself to hear that which is said, learn. Teach others that which helped, that which hurt, and make any weakness a new found strength from which to move forward as your journey continues!

LEARN THE GOOD WHEN THINGS GO BAD, for maybe, just maybe, the angels amongst us helped YOU realize your blessings before those blessings were gone!

There are steps to be taken, for WE are to move on, shall WE begin?

38. IT WAS NOT THEIR PLAN TO DIE FOR OUR NATION . . .

It was not THEIR plan to die for OUR Nation, for OUR Brothers and Sisters in the Service that have FALLEN, had dreams too, had families too, had HOPE for a FUTURE that was better, safer, long, and prosperous! They would move on to that which would come next, confident and assured that others would follow in their footsteps, serving "WE", being as vigilant, confident, prepared to do that which "WE asked of them".

That they died as a consequence of their decision to serve, knowing the risk and the possibility, and yet, still they served US with HONOR. Their death denying fulfillment of dreams, denying family and friend of their presence in life that would follow, such decision, such sacrifice on OUR behalf DEMANDS OUR acknowledgement at least for a "day", one day out of 365!

IS THAT TOO UCH TO ASK OF "US"? Can WE not HONOR THEM, as THEY have HONORED US with that which THEY have sacrificed?

There is a movie, available on demand, on dvd, in stores entitled "TAKING CHANCE" (starring Kevin Bacon, HBO films). It is the true story of one Marines final trip HOME from war, to US, accompanied by another Marine in search of answers. I urge YOU, my fellow Countrymen, PLEASE watch that movie this weekend with family, with friend, so that on Monday, Memorial Day, WE all can truly understand and better appreciate the sacrifices made on OUR behalf!

Although YOU will be saddened at first, the strength that YOU will realize aware of the blessings that WE all share, will enrich YOUR HEART, and fuel the fires within YOU to LIVE FREE.

OUR flag before YOU waving against blue sky will take on a much grander meaning, and not enough words of thanks will be able to come from your lips!

How do WE HONOR the FALLEN? By living as WE were meant to live; ". . . FREE at last . . .", by finding the PASSION that burns within each of US, pursuing it relentlessly, daring to be different, daring to be true, daring to be bold, by DARING TO BE YOU!

There is so much to do. There is so much that can be done. WE as a People, as a Nation, can DO BETTER! Is not the sacrifice of OUR FALLEN worthy of OUR effort?

Like THEM, I believe in YOU, I believe in ME, I believe in WE, and WE CAN DO BETTER! Shall WE begin?

39. IS FAITH, IS FAMILY, IS LOVE NECESSARY/

Is FAITH necessary? Absolutely, without any question nor hesitation FAITH is essential to "LIFE". Does not your finger or toe require your thought commanding it to move? You think such a thought because you believe with the expectation that such a thought will be answered with the desired result, movement so desired. You believed because you had FAITH. Your FAITH empowered you; to think, to imagine what could be, what would be, what will be, to decide, to act, to persevere, adapt if necessary, and overcome any difficulty and continue until the desired action was accomplished, your finger or toe moved!

Is not FAITH necessary for each of us to believe that we as individuals are significant, that we as individuals do have a purpose for being, that our being and doing is of some consequence to those around us, the World around us, the life before us? With such FAITH in us, are we not then capable of looking within our minds and our hearts and finding that passion that burns as bright as the Sun within us to pursue, and while so doing enrich ourselves and all around us, as well as our World at the same time? Have not we, US, OUR WORLD benefited? There lies the significance for being!

With such belief in our significance, in our purpose, is not our FAITH strengthened, empowering us to think, to imagine what could be, what would be, what will be next, to decide, to act to be not alone but to have FAITH in another as well, and further to have FAITH in what will happen when two become one, and a child is conceived. Our FAITH fostered LIFE, and with that LIFE, renewal, strengthening our FAITH even further in our hopes and prayers for tomorrow, empowering US; to think, to imagine what could be, what would be, what will be, to decide, to act, to persevere, adapt if necessary and overcome any difficulty, and to continue until the desired outcome is accomplished! Is FAITH necessary? What say YOU?

Is Family necessary? Whether you believe it or not, whether you think it or not, FAMILY is necessary, for WE are not alone, and OUR existence is of consequence one way or another. We are of the same family, the FAMILY of man, therefore WE impact the WORLD around us in some similar fashion. The use of resources, over development / underdevelopment, moderation, conflict, confrontation, exploration, exploitation, balance, harmony, all results of choices we make as individuals, and as the FAMILY of man!

When we as individuals have FAITH in another, when two become one, and child is conceived, does not each have FAITH in the other to do that which they believe is necessary for the life of their child, life of their family, life of their World in which they, WE, are a part? Would not it benefit your brother's family, your sister's family, your neighbor's family, the FAMILY of man, OUR WORLD, to have similar FAITH in them? So empowered would WE be; to think, to imagine what could be, what would be, what will be, to decide, to act, to persevere, to adapt if necessary and overcome any difficulty, to forgive, and to continue until OUR desired outcome is accomplished! Is FAITH necessary, is FAMILY necessary? What say you?

Is LOVE necessary? With FAITH empowering us, we looked within our minds and hearts and found our passion, our purpose burning bright as the Sun, and chose to pursue it relentlessly, enriching all around us and the World in which we live. Our realization of our significance further strengthened our FAITH, empowering US to further LIFE expanding FAMILY. LOVE is the elastic bond that allows us as individuals, and as a FAMILY to endure that which is painful, difficult, unnerving, and pulls us back sometimes from the brink to solid ground of our FAITH. Love is the elastic bond that allows us as individuals, and as a FAMILY to be tethered and pulled back to reality from the lofty heights of perceived importance or success, and to once again stand on solid ground firm in FAITH! LOVE will always find a way, given the opportunity, and that opportunity arises from FAITH, from FAMILY.

Is FAITH necessary, is FAMILY necessary, is LOVE necessary? What say YOU? Isn't it worth finding out?

I have FAITH in YOU, I have FAITH in ME, I have FAITH in WE! Believe, WE are not alone nor will WE ever be! Shall WE begin?

40. "ATTITUDE OF GRATITUDE"

First a special note; I had written this piece on Facebook, untitled, for all to see, to share in the joy, and in the hope to inspire others to pursue that which calls from within their heart. Love truly knows no bounds; whether it be for family, friend, GOD and / or country, purpose or pursuit. There is a reason for YOUR being, have FAITH and BELIEVE, hear that which calls from within YOUR heart and DARE TO BE YOU! I thank one of my High School classmates, a friend of many years, George Gelish for providing me with too good a title to not to have put to use when writing this. And so to George I say; "Thank-you, and may YOUR 30th Anniversary in the coming days be ever so joyful, fill your heart, and delight your Soul!

"ATTITUDE OF GRATITUDE"—written June 22, 2013

Yesterday, June 21st, I celebrated my 27th wedding anniversary with my wife Diane, and I realized how very fortunate, and how well blessed I have been, especially having had her in my life all these years.

Today, as I went about my chores, my tasks, I could not thank God enough for the wealth I have come to realize; the love of my wife, having witnessed and shared the growth and transition of our children from little ones to the wonderful adults they have come to be, and of whom their significant others have further enriched our hearts and delighted our minds. I never dreamt of a wealth "so grand" as "that which now fills my heart and Soul because of her love, and the love of family".

As a result, now more than ever before, I wish and pray that God will so bless each of YOU, friend, and family, to experience such wealth, for it is truly Heaven while on Earth!

It is so worth doing, so worth the effort, the perseverance, the patience, the trial, the mistakes, the successes, so worth believing and achieving! Love truly does find a way! Knowing what I know now, if I could, I wouldn't change one step that I've taken up to now, for I might not have arrived at where I am right now!

Each day beyond today, each new memory shared and experienced, is but the icing atop the perfect cake!

DARE TO BE YOU, for YOU are magnificent, and so shall YOUR Life be! Have FAITH, BELIEVE, surrender YOUR Heart to LOVE and be amazed at that which WILL BE!

YOUR time has come, let YOUR LOVE show YOU the way, it will not fail YOU nor will GOD above!

41. THANK GOD FOR FACEBOOK, AND THAT WHICH IS NOW POSSIBLE!

To those of YOU who are young, a World without the Internet could not be imagined, and yet, because of the Internet, and the technology that you are already accustomed to daily, you imagine that "which can and someday will be, without boundaries nor limitations, for anything appears to be possible given time and effort".

To the now grown children of Baby-boomers, YOU have witnessed the emergence of technology on a scale unparalleled in the History of man. You have been on the front line and continually tasked with the responsibility of making that which is new, routine, socially and ethically responsible and acceptable to the World of old, and to the World in which your children now come.

To the aging Baby-boomers, most of whom who can still vividly remember being tethered to 6 foot telephone handset cords, and having to have phone conversations overheard by near everyone in the family because "the phone" was in the central area of the house most commonly used throughout the day and night, the speed with which communication can now travel, and to the places it can now reach, can at times, near make US believe WE are dreaming, and not awake!

You of Youth, and those who embrace and accept that which now is, a World technologically advanced and connected, have advantages at your fingertips, that if used for good, can allow Humanity to advance also, as never before!

For never does a child, a young adult, a single parent, a handicapped person nor an isolated elderly person, EVER have to feel or be alone again; Help, guidance, companionship is but a click away (even if on the other side of the Earth).

Thank God for Facebook and social media; for if used for good, the benefits to family and friend, to Nation, to Country, to Humanity, to the World in which WE are a part, are limitless!

When Baby-boomers grew, and for whatever the reason or cause, as families fractured or moved apart, often lines of communication were nonexistent, and the strength of family could seem lost or weakened.

But now, all who embrace, and accept that which is possible because of the Internet and social media, all can be connected to those so loved, those so needed, those so valuable a part of OUR Life. Hopes and dreams, experiences of young and old can be shared with the clarity, and certainty of the Sun rising each morning. Family and friends can share moments of their lives while still pursuing that which must be done, from where it must be done, all with but a click on a mouse!

Heartache, and sorrow, triumph or tragedy, all can be shared by the peoples of the World in which WE live. Love of family, of friend, of a cause, of a pursuit can be shared in the blink of an eye, no strings attached!

FREEDOM and JUSTICE can be witnessed by all, and HUMANITY can address that which is now wrong, timely! LOVE can find a way to strengthen the hearts and minds of many, FAITH and BELIEF can be shared and understood. HOPE restored. Thankfulness experienced and shared by all!

So use that which is available for good, learn it, master it, embrace it, for OUR WORLD will be all the better for it!

Shall WE begin?

42. THIS MORNING I HAD THE OPPORTUNITY . . .

This morning (Wed. July 17th), I had the opportunity to be of assistance to a man who lives on the streets. When I came upon him, he was resting on a piece of cardboard laid out beneath a construction scaffold (he was using it to shade himself from the rising Sun).

It's been brutally HOT in the city (New York) these days, and when I handed him water bottles, and a sleeve of Ritz crackers, he looked at me like he had won the lottery. As I shook his hand, I couldn't help noticing how warm he felt, and how very swollen his bare feet were.

I reached into my backpack and took out a package of "WET ONES" (damp citrus scented cleaning wipes). I showed him how to take them out of the pack, and how to re-seal it so they would stay damp.

No sooner than I had taken the first wipe out filling the air around us with an orange scent, when he startled me with what he said; "That smells like my wife!" He said she had passed away "a long time ago, and that it was nice to smell her again!"

He was so happy to rub them on his skin and cool off a bit! He was so happy!

All it took was a few minutes of my time, a few bottles of water (I gave him one more before I left), a pack of "WET ONES", a sleeve of Ritz crackers, a shake of a hand, a willingness and a want to hear what he had to say!

It was a nice way to continue on my way, and afforded me once again, a reason to count my blessings, and to give thanks to GOD.

I try to do at least one Random Act of Kindness on my way "in" to work, and at least one on my way home from work each day. I dedicate each act to my fellow Marines that have "FALLEN", as my way to never forget their sacrifice, and to honor them.

It's a wonderful way for YOU too, to remember and honor someone that may have passed. Give it a go, it sure can't hurt, and YOU may really like how YOU feel!!!!

Shall WE begin?

43. WHEN OPPORTUNITY KNOCKS, NOT ONLY THE GOOD ANSWER

Being a parent, with now grown children in their twenties, and thirties, as I commute to and from New York City at a variety of times, I notice with frequency, how often other grown children place themselves in harm's way because they are; "turned in" to something else via electronic device or worse, because they are drunk or in "altered state".

Granted the hours I arrive in NYC's Penn Station (between 4:45am to 5:30am), and I am out on the streets (5:30-6:15am) would be a factor most certainly, but danger is very real, very present, and given the opportunity, just a matter of time before it finds YOU.

Two noteworthy examples this week; the first involving a young woman who could not have been two or three years older then my own daughter. Her voice and her manner caught the attention of many of us from afar as we neared to pass while on our way to work. Clearly she was petrified of a Pimp who was trying ever so calmly to get her to return to him and exit the station immediately. She was resisting, by taking one step deeper into the station for each step he took in her direction. But closer did he get because his steps were bigger as he advanced told her, and she backed away. Her eyes would tear further as he advanced, and witnessing it all, were people rendered helpless because no crime was being committed in their presence. But those who have been around, who knew these streets, who knew the signs of danger to come, "knew" that when she left with him, well it was going to be a "very bad day"!

In minutes, hundreds had passed the two continuing on their way, and praying for a happy outcome. There was none! I saw her again on my way home 14 hours later a block from the station, on a crowded city street during rush hour with people returning "home". She had two black eyes, bruised cheeks, wearing barely nothing in the frigid rain, and her day was probably just starting anew!

The other; by her clothes and how well kept she had been, she most likely had gone out partying with her friends the night before, and at some point, was attempting to make her way home to somewhere on Long Island. She had bought pizza and a drink to eat on the train or while waiting for it. At some point, she sat down on the ultra wide staircase from the platforms to the lobby about 7 feet up from the bottom step, for that is where her belongings were, her purse, her pizza, her drink, her coat. She must've gotten sick to her stomach and leaned forward to puke (because it was everywhere), and then probably passed out falling face down into it, and then slide down a little further in it, feet now up the stairs, head near the bottom, legs wide open exposing her undergarments to all who passed.

The train had near a thousand people on it, and when the doors opened, there was the mad dash for the ultra wide staircase which came to an abrupt halt. The volume of noise of so many approaching woke the young lady, and as she attempted to right herself, she slipped and fell again into the pool of vomit. Some offered a hand, as did I, but she, out of embarrassment, would not accept our help. Within two minutes she would be alone again. I prayed for her to get home safe, and thanked GOD that the trash (pimps and hoodlums) one flight up, was not aware she had even been there. They would have had a field day stealing her belongings, if not something else!

Two extremes, two completely different circumstances, two polar opposites, and yet similarities abound, for they too were someone's daughter, and they too were in Penn Station, as is mine daily, as YOURS may be as well!

Please, please be mindful of your surroundings, and safeguard yourself and those with you as best you can, always. Tune in to the life that greets you each day, DARE TO BE YOU, and if opportunity presents itself for you to assist another on their way, then please help them without endangering yourself (call the police). Have a great day!

P.S.—Have YOU talked to YOUR grown children lately? Now would be a good time! Shall WE begin?

44. ON "THE DAY" YOU FEEL LOST, ABANDONED, TORN OR BROKEN

Again, a friend asked me; "Why do YOU (me) write so much about FAITH, about BELIEF? Don't YOU want people to read things YOU have written? Aren't YOU afraid of being labeled or thought of as some GOD nut?"

Well, I was shocked, and honestly, disappointed, for clearly the person did not know me or really care to (not many do "know me", and normally, from experience, it is "I" that has learned to keep distance between myself and others to lessen the hurt when and if they pass before me, as did my fellow Marines, that pain was and is excruciating for me still today).

For you see, for any, any relationship to develop, to have meaning, both parties involved have to give and receive, which means allow others to give back to you. Since the death of my fellow Marines, and the circumstances of their death in the Beirut Airport bombing Oct 1983, I could count the number of people I've allowed "in" solely on my two hands, and still have unused fingers (my wife Diane, my stepson Joe, his significant other Theresa, my son Michael, his significant other Michelle, my daughter Anna Lynn, and her significant other Danny). They are my World, and I have allowed them into my very Soul (as have they, let me in)!

Outside of them, I give myself freely and absolutely in every possible way to assist others, to encourage others, to inspire others, but then I move on, for I know my time is short.

It is because of that, that I write so often about FAITH, about BELIEF, I am here by the Will of GOD, and if not for HIS WILL, neither would I be here. I never would've met my wife nor my stepson, my children would not have been born, and none of them and "their significant others" would've entered into our minds, our hearts, our Souls. In loving them, in being loved by them, I have discovered and been blessed with a wealth beyond compare to last all eternity!

Being the youngest in my birth family, separate at first by many years of age, and by illness within the family, a loving environment, yet dysfunctional, when I joined the Marines I found my way, a road to travel that challenged me, intrigued me, excited me, beckoned me. School after school, unit after unit, I leapfrogged my way into my Marine Family of RECON MARINES, and for much of my seven years, found HOME. Then, GONE in minutes Oct 23rd 1983.

My specific reenlistment request (for my third tour, I wanted revenge against those guilty, so I wanted the opportunity to be with the unit I assumed would be given the orders to go get them), was denied (because of my desire for revenge), but every other option and duty would be approved (for "I was the Marines Marine, a Lifer if there was ever a Lifer", and such was my reputation).

Pissed off beyond belief, devastated that I was denied the opportunity to "serve Justice", haunted by the knowledge that I was not by their side when blown to bits or crushed by tons of collapsing concrete (because I was not there), haunted by their ghosts, I separated from service. When asked what I would do, I answered; "Flip hamburgers at a burger place in my hometown". Which is exactly what I did, and I even had a Polaroid picture taken of me doing just that and sent it to them in the hopes it would piss them off (but I'm sure it didn't, they probably were more of the mind "what a waste").

But the reality of the situation was this; I WAS LOST, THE MOST LOST I HAVE EVER BEEN, THE MOST ALONE I HAVE BEEN WITHIN MIND AND HEART!

I was home, in the house I grew up in, but it was as if I was on another planet in a different time, NOTHING mattered!

But from within me, from way down deep, way down beyond thought of mind or heart, a stirring from within my Soul urging me to ask for help, not just any help, but help from GOD above. You see, always have I been firm in my FAITH and my BELIEF in GOD, always had my prayers of past been answered. Such was the call from deep within me that day, for I "KNEW" even from the edge of the abyss, that "IF" I asked for HIS help to find my way, well, my prayers would be answered. I asked!

HE ANSWERED!

"Two days later, I was out of the hamburger place and interviewing for a job in Inventory Control Management with a Computer Supply Company. Although many applied and were interviewed, I got the job that day!

I met a few people there (Diane was one of them), and a group of us would go out to eat lunch together almost daily.

30 minutes a day that helped to heal a broken heart, for it rekindled a childhood dream of meeting "the right girl, falling in love, marrying her, and having a family of our own to love, protect, and provide for".

That dream had been shattered years earlier while I was in the service and came home unannounced and found the woman I thought that would happen with, with another. That result, I turned completely towards my training as a RECON MARINE with no looking back. RECON MARINES became my Family, and OUR mission, my purpose, my reason for being!

While our lunches continued, and I enjoyed doing my work, at night, I furthered my studies in Engineering. Come the holidays (Christmas), I got up the nerve to ask Diane to go to the Company Holiday Party with me. She agreed, but we both decided to meet at the location by driving in separate cars.

Shortly thereafter, we moved in together, then got married, and have been together ever since. So, once again GOD saved me, how could I not BELIEVE, how could I not have FAITH ! Did not my life do an abrupt 360?

So armed, so blessed, how could I not assist others and honor my FALLEN Marines at the same time by doing anything I could to be of service, to inspire, to encourage, to help others in need. Always do I stand for another, and always will I speak of FAITH, of BELIEF, so that on "THE DAY" when YOU or anyone else is in need of them, they are there!

I use every means possible to get that message across, and to reach every possible group of people (that's why I post stories, videos, music, poetry). I have been shown the way for me, and I have chosen to DARE TO BE ME by inspiring others positively through my written words, through My Random Acts of Kindness (MyR.A.K.), by being the best I can possibly be, doing the absolute most of that which I can do, and that has made a World of difference. There are Angels here amongst us, to help us, to guide us, for my wife Diane is surely one of them, and each and every day I praise GOD for having sent her and Joseph into my life!

But WE, YOU and I together, and all others, strengthened by OUR Angels, by our love of and for Family, can do better still!

Is not OUR World worth OUR most sincere effort? Should not OUR last words be of thanks and praise to GOD for having blessed US as HE has?

WE have nothing to lose, but ETERNITY to gain! Shall WE begin?

Note: You can read more about the highlight of the Company Holiday Party night in an earlier piece entitled "HEAR THE MUSIC, FEEL THE BEAT . . . CHOOSE TO DANCE", #29 IN THIS BOOK.

45. HOW WILL YOU HANDLE A LIFE ALTERING EVENT?

How will YOU handle a LIFE ALTERING EVENT? "WITH FAITH", and "ONE STEP AT A TIME"!

GOD never gives US more than WE can handle, HE just knows US better than WE often know OURSELVES!

When faced with a LIFE ALTERING EVENT: A birth, a death, an illness, an injury, LOVE, lust, dream or desire, when passion seems to beckon each and every waking moment; "Have FAITH, BELIEVE, ask for guidance, and in time, HIS way will be seen, a path unique unto YOU, to be chosen by YOU and YOU alone!

The choice is YOURS to make, but NEVER shall HE fail YOU!

Armed with FAITH, with BELIEF, NEVER EVER will YOU walk alone! There will HE be, there will HIS Angels be, there will YOUR GUARDIANS be to lift YOU, to protect YOU, to comfort YOU, to strengthen YOU and YOUR resolve to GO ON! There will HE BE, WITH YOU!

HOW WILL I HANDLE A LIFE ALTERING EVENT? As I do now, with my FAITH and BELIEF in GOD, taking ONE STEP AT A TIME FOR AS LONG AS I MUST, for that is my choice!

Won't YOU choose the same? The choice is YOURS to make, but NEVER, EVER shall YOU walk alone!

Shall WE begin?

46. THE WAY TO RECOVERY, TO HEAL A WOUNDED OR FEARFUL HEART . . .

The way to recovery, to heal a wounded or fearful heart, is to embrace that which is good, that which is honorable, that which is heroic!

Amidst the hours of chaos, confusion, and uncertainty resulting from the horrorific events of this week (the Boston Marathon Bombing and the pursuit of those responsible, and the Texas Fertilizer Plant Fire and explosion), heroes emerged from within OUR ranks of "WE the People", fellow countrymen who ventured into that which all wished had NEVER been. Many were trained, some were not, but answer the call to serve, to protect, to help, to heal, to assist others of US (WE), in OUR time and place of need.

May the stories of the HEALING HANDS, the outpouring of endless love flood the social media, the press, and serve to rekindle, awaken the spark within those still in shock. It is to the heights to which WE NOW climb, from the depths of which WE have been, that Liberty's Bell of Freedom will ring, and "the WORLD WILL SING".

For FREEDOM is in the hearts and minds the WORLD over, and it IS OURS that they most often dream of and attempt to emulate!

I believe in YOU, I believe in ME, I believe in WE, "WE the People", a People United, that will stand in the Face of that which is bad, champion that which is good, embracing LIFE, LIBERTY, the PURSUIT of HAPPINESS by daring to be TRUE to that which is within mind and heart, mindful of that which calls from the hearts and minds of others, by having the courage to STAND when others cannot, by looking in the morning mirror and saying;

"DARE TO BE YOU, FOR YOU ARE SIGNIFICANT!" As are WE all!

There is much to be done, SHALL WE BEGIN?

47. HURRAH, IT'S BACK TO SCHOOL TIME, IT'S TIME TO LEARN!!!

Like the World of Nature looks forward to Spring, the opportunity for NEW LIFE, fresh beginnings, near limitless possibilities, so do I always look forward to the new school year!

Why? Think about it; Millions and millions of humans begin to focus their minds on knowledge, on creativity, on discovery, on finding solutions, on their pursuit of dreams, on making that which was but an idea, REALITY! How cool is that!

And no matter what OUR age or where WE are, whether at home on land, sea, or orbiting the Earth, WE can still participate, for WE can choose to learn!

I love it, even the thought of it, and I sure do hope YOU do as well, there's nothing stopping YOU or me! With the wonderful world of technology at OUR fingertips 24/7, WE have flexibility like never before, access to sources the World over, and convenience to do what must be done when WE have time.

Whether you're learning about something you love, something you know little about, something of importance or something trivial, if YOU absorb and retain even a mere 10% (but more likely 70-80%), the benefits to YOU, to HUMANITY, can be unbelievable!

Can YOU imagine if YOU picked up a book or read an article that YOU may have otherwise never picked up, and after reading mere sentences, something clicked on within YOUR mind and heart, something called out to YOU from within almost screaming; "This is for YOU, this is great! I want to do this, learn this!" And, as a result, YOU found YOUR LIFE'S work, YOUR PASSION, AND YOU CHOSE RIGHT THEN TO PURSUE IT!

Even if YOUR passion, YOUR purpose wasn't yet discovered, with each new thing learned the opportunities to enrich YOUR life, to advance, to grasp, to understand the World around YOU, US is better, and yes the possibility of taking one more step closer towards that which is within YOUR mind and heart yet to be discovered is greater! Is that bad? I think not, but YOU are the one who needs to answer!

Because YOU do construction, plumbing, are a Fireman, Policeman, a Serviceman here at home or overseas, a receptionist, a doctor or a lawyer, a lifeguard at a pool, none of those things define YOU, limit YOU, prevent YOU from learning for LIFE, for discovering the passion and the purpose within YOU. Obviously if YOUR passion and purpose was already discovered, is being pursued, more can always be learned to YOUR benefit and OUR World in which YOU are a part, for YOU ARE SIGNIFICANT!

I love back to school time because the air, the atmosphere is alive with ENERGY unleashed, and the possibilities of that which may come as a result, truly LIMITLESS!

So learn a language, learn to dance, learn the power of a single VOICE, learn to STAND when others sit, learn to LISTEN, and maybe YOU'LL hear, the VOICE within YOU is NOW HERE!

DARE TO BE DIFFERENT, DARE TO BE TRUE, DARE TO BE BOLD, DARE TO BE YOU! You are magnificent, and OUR WORLD is all the better for YOU ARE HERE!

There's much to be done, SHALL WE BEGIN?

48. A WONDERFULLY ENLIGHTENING LESSON FOR YOU TO LEARN!

Quite a wonderful lesson did I learn while a resident at Island Nursing Home and Rehab Center in Holtsville, NY. Gone are my misconceptions of life within such a facility, gone are my beliefs that such a place is where the elderly or disabled are dropped off to be forgotten, for nothing could be further from the truth (at least not at this facility)!

From the moment I arrived after what I would have thought to be normal business hours, I was greeted warmly and assisted in every possible way. With respect for privacy, and patience for my modesty, it was explained how and why an initial evaluation of the condition of the rest of body was important to document in what condition I did arrive, so that progress could also be documented correctly in the coming days.

Such gentleness, such caring, such respect was shown, in minutes I was so at ease that my wife and I had made the right decision to have me go to INRC (especially since it was so near home and family)!

Once the evaluation was done, and necessities taken care of, food was provided, medications given, a visit form family, and then lights out.

The first night was eventful because the routine and the sounds were new; there were residents in many a varied state, some requiring greater assistance than others to do what to you on the "outside" would think simple tasks, but to "us" (in weakened condition), are monumental, requiring near Herculean strength, and the patience of the angels of mercy assisting us. With patience, with kindess, with strength and grace, each of us was assisted in the manner necessary.

As the night progressed, as the calm settled in, you could hear machines in the distance, you could hear voices in normal conversation, you could hear the night nurse making her rounds giving medications, taking vitals, giving soothing words of encouragement. You could hear a resident or two awakened in fright, only to be calmed well before daylight.

The first morning came and awake was I in a flash, help did I need to the tiolet so I would not crash. So humbling was it for me once again, as it was in the hospital, to require assistance to get to and then to sit down on "the toilet" (something you have done near a million timeson your own before weakened state). Modesty aside, when you have got to go, you have to go, and modesty goes out the window, especially when you need help getting your shorts down and then up again. What previously would have taken 2 or 3 minutes with no sweat, now was an exhausting procedure that could've also been life's most humiliating as well, but it wasn't!

So wonderfully was I assisted, beyond mere professionally, but with caring and compassion (as I witnessed all others being treated as well). But boy, returning to bed "never looked so good"!

With food in my belly, washed, dressings changed, and dressed, all the first full day formalities were then addressed; admin paperwork, physical therapy / occupational therapy evaluation, vitals taken, medications taken, equipment delivered (walker, wheelchair, hip kit consisting of devices to assist you in carrying out daily tasks), visits from Doctor, Social Worker, Administrator, greetings from day shift, lab techs.

Assistance with the necessities, time and time again (toilet / washing).

Lunch served, more visits, decisions made, visits by family, dinner served, medications, more assistance with necessities (damn was I worn out, and I hadn't even started any therapy yet, although I had a wonderful lesson teaching me how to use devices to help me pull up my own shorts, put on my own socks without bending, and wash spots I couldn't see or previously reach), more visits by family, more medications, then lights out. This time, with the sounds now growing familiar, and exhausted, I fell asleep with greater ease.

The next day, my second full day, things became routine, a schedule had been made and was being followed. The day was predictable, and precise. People were met, conversations took place, therapy took center stage, and much progress was made.

Each day there progressed exactly the same way for me, for that was my routine, as others had their routine!

I witnessed and marveled at the care and attention being paid to each and every resident. I welcomed the sense of purpose, the enthusiasm displayed by staff and residents. The simplest progress was welcomed by all, and the smiles were as glorious and warm as the rays of the Sun. Seeing the smiles upon the faces of the elderly, warmed my heart so. So very joyful were they with even the slightest acknowledgement as to that which "they accomplished". It was wonderful to witness, and inspired me to work as hard as I could, to smile as much as I could, to greet each person I could, to praise each person I could.

I marveled at the way each therapist added their own personality into assisting others, the touch of a hand, a smile on their face, a timely word, a pat on the back. Demanding were they, and pushed did they, but never for a second did you think not who they were there for, YOU!

I couldn't wait for lunch to be done, necessities taken care of, and to return to round two with the Physical Therapists / Occupational Therapists. Never was I disappointed!

I got to see more of daily life in the facility, more of the services afforded the residents; in house Doctor, Dentist, Beauty / Barber Shop, clothes cleaning service, religious services, day-rooms for visiting with residents, friends or family, bingo, creative writing sessions, event nights with comedy shows, movies, football games on big screens (taped, in case on too late) or live. I saw support staff time and time again going well beyond their assigned tasks in a manner that exhibited true caring and real compassion for residents, and for other staff they assisted. Such an environment does not happen by accident, it takes effort, sincere effort daily by all. Credit must be given to all, and shared by all. I got to see a community of people, where people cared about other people (staff to staff, staff to resident, resident to staff, resident to resident). It was wonderful, and "so not anticipated", but so very warmly regarded and accepted as fact!

I saw the bent and the broken in mind and body awakened to a new state of being, renewed with passion for life "as it would be" (be it for short or long).

That being the case, I ask YOU this; "Are not the hands of all working and living in such a place HEALING HANDS, for are not those that have helped, healed as well with that which THEY too have gained?" And if that be the case, has not GOD'S HAND been at work as well?

Clearly, WE are all different, but significant are WE all! DARE TO BE DIFFERENT, DARE TO BE TRUE, DARE TO BE BOLD, DARE TO BE YOU!

OUR World is all the better for YOU being YOU, and doing that which YOU are passionate and capable of doing! And in YOUR pursuit many a person's path do YOU cross or perhaps share for a time or two, might not YOUR HANDS be HEALING HANDS as well? And if that is the case, how are YOU not significant in even more ways than YOU might have imagined? And if THAT be the case, has not GOD'S HAND been at work for YOU as well?

Is not OUR World all the better for "US" being active within it? Shall WE begin?

49. REMEMBER WHERE WE WERE AS SANDY'S WATERS ROSE?

On this day, the one year anniversary of the arrival of Super-storm Sandy in the Tri-state area of New York, New Jersey, and Connecticut, much can be said for the resilience of the human spirit when so battered and beaten down not once, but multiple times, and in so many a varied way!

Previously, in the same month of October 2012, WE had already been belted by a Tropical Storm that had soaked the ground, risen ground water tables to astronomical heights, caused most catch basins to remain full long after the storm moved away. With the ground so soft, even the slightest breeze toppled shallow rooted trees, blocked roads, crushed vehicles and houses, knocked down power lines causing fires and outages as temperatures dropped. Misery in the form of no power, no heat, massive commuter delays, and disruptions was "just a prelude" to "that which in a couple of weeks" would and "did" become the grandest of knockout punches for millions of "WE"!

All of US in the Tri-state, and even the majority across the Land WE so love, know only too well, the devastation, the destruction, the pain, the suffering, the loss of LIFE, of livelihood, of LIFE as it had been known, that came next, and with "just the approach of Super Storm Sandy!" When the storm actually arrived, so vivid are all the news reports, photos, and stories imprinted within OUR minds and burned within OUR hearts! As the winds gained strength, as the waters rose, HELL had shown a new face, and nowhere was there to run!!!

Thousands of even the strongest trees fell, whole trains were swept away off their tracks, amusement parks were swept out to Sea, highways became raging rivers and then lakes, varied man created systems labeled "never to fail" were gone as if in a blink, and millions of people, of US, were in shock and denial, pleading with GOD to please wake US up from this nightmare WE must be having! But WE weren't!!!!! Damn!!!!!!

Nature in her fury has but no equal except but for GOD'S amazing GRACE when lives are spared, for all else means nothing, is of no use, no purpose, if there is no one left alive!

When all is said and done, after all the images and stories digested, even after the realization that still now, one year later, many people are without their home, so very much do WE have to be thankful for, for WE LIVE!

And WE have been given a gift, a gift so magnificent that no price can even be put upon it, and each of US has it in a place from which it cannot be taken from US without OUR consent, for it is within OUR heart! It is the power to HEAL!

If YOU do not believe, I only need to remind YOU of those very same images, and stories, and suggest YOU compare them against that which YOU see now; LOOK, for today will WE be flooded with that which was then, and that WHICH NOW IS!

Herculean effort, resourcefulness beyond compare, unprecedented innovation, bipartisanship on the grandest of scales proving compromise and solution can truly be found "when" so willed by "WE"!

Yes, no question, there "IS" more still to be done, for many are without their home, their livelihood, relief from HELL!

And so now do I ask each and every one to be mindful of the gift "WE" have been given, the gift to HEAL, and to use it, for ourselves, and for others of "WE". For each and every one of US is significant, and WE all have HANDS that can HEAL if WE listen to that which is within OUR heart and "do that which WE are capable of doing".

I believe in YOU, I believe in ME, I believe in "WE the People"! Let US HEAL from within OUR hearts, and reach out as best WE can! Let US HEAL OUR towns, cities, States, Nation!

DARE TO BE DIFFERENT, DARE TO BE TRUE, DARE TO BE BOLD, DARE TO BE YOU!

So much is there still to do! Shall WE begin?

50. NEED YOU BE ASHAMED OR EMBARRASSED FOR THAT WHICH "YOU CAN DO"

The amount of good that can be done by one person is remarkable, so many factors come into play, but the greatest factor of all is reliant most assuredly upon this; "Doing that which YOU are capable of doing, taking action, DOING!"

This quote truly helps to inspire and make clear how very significant each person cn be "if" they "DO" what they are capable of doing;

"I am only one, but still I am one. I cannot do everything, but still I can do something; and because I cannot do everything, I will not refuse to do the something that I can do". —EDWARD EVERETT HALE

Just like every journey, no matter the length, must start with "the first step", so too does every task, every endeavor, every dream destined to become reality, it must begin!

If the desire is to help someone in need, that which "is available to be given" will be well received because it helps to fill the need (regardless of size), progress is made in the right direction with the action taken. Your action might even be the first, the catalyst that opens the flood gate of additional assistance that might never have come without YOU having taken action, DOING that which YOU were capable of doing!

Most of US have heard some version of the story about the Statue of Liberty being a gift to America bought and paid for by "the pennies of children". There is some truth to it, and "their pennies" did play a significant role in ultimately getting the statue to stand where it does now in fact stand, Liberty Island upon its pedestal.

The idea of the Statue to be made and given to America as a gift from France was from a French Political Figure and known writer named Edouard de Laboulaye. It was to be a gift meant to celebrate Liberty.

A French sculptor namedFedric Auguste Bartholdi took the time to design the potential statue, and went further promoting the idea.

But how to pay for it? A question that arises about everything and anything to be done, then, and now for US as well! Well then, the first people interested in seriously promoting the statue in 1875 became known as the French American Union. To raise money, they asked for donations; from the people of France for the statue, and from the people of America for construction of the base / pedestal upon which the statue would stand.

The story about "pennies from children paying for the statue" was partly correct; because French school children were allowed to, and did in fact, donate "what they could" (often, mere cents / pennies, was what they could give).

The majority of the French donations for the statue came from people in over 180 towns, villages, cities. As the pieces of the statue arrived in America and were displayed, interest increased and news stories started to circulate. Americans started to donate slowly. When American newspapers played up th story about French School children donating their pennies, Americans more generously opened their purses and their wallets, and sufficient funds were collected to pay for the construction of the base / Pedestal upon which the statue does in fact stand today.

Clearly, someone on both sides of the ocean had to be "the first one" to donate; in France for the statue, in America for the base / pedestal. The first donation might have been pennies or huge (for that time) on both sides of the ocean. The result is now visible for

US all to see every time WE look at Liberty Island in New York, there Lady Liberty stands!

And so before US lies the significance and the simplicity of that quote read above; "I am only one, but still am I one. I cannot do everything, but still I can do something; and because I cannot do everything, I WILL NOT REFUSE TO DO THE SMETHING THAT I CAN DO." —EDWARD EVERETT HALE

Let not US refuse to do the something each of US can do when, and if the time comes, when the need comes; be it mere pennies in our pocket or "signing a blank check saying UP to and including payment with my life" (as is the case when serving OUR Nation in the Armed Services).

Each and every one of US is significant, for WE have been the granted the miracle of LIFE, WE are here. WE have purpose, a reason for being. When WE as individuals look within our mind and heart, we will find our passion, our purpose! When YOU find YOURS, as I have already, pursue it as best YOU possibly can, for OUR WORLD is all the better for it, and OUR being in it!

And along OUR way, if by chance another WE could assist, make available that "which we are capable of giving, be it mere pennies or our life's work, and in so "doing", have not WE helped? And if WE have helped, have not OUR HANDS HEALED?

And if that be so, have not WE honored GOD in Heaven for the miracle of OUR Birth? Has not HIS HAND been at work all the while?

WE are all significant, each and every one, hear that which calls from within YOUR heart and choose to listen! DARE TO BE DIFFERENT, DARE TO BE TRUE, DARE TO BE BOLD, DARE TO BE YOU!

THERE BEFORE US, OUR PATH AWAITS, SHALL WE BEGIN?

51. "WHAT HAVE YOU GOT TO LOSE IF YOU ARE . . ."

Six days into the New Year, have YOU given your resolutions a chance to be fulfilled? Have YOU thrown them out the window? Did you even make any? Do you laugh at the thought or the people (friends and family) that make them every year, and know they won't do anything to fulfill them? Does it matter? Should it matter?

What matters are the people making the resolutions, for whatever the reason(s), for they, are WE (maybe YOU, maybe ME, but one or more of WE), and WE are the People of this Nation, and the Peoples of other Nations, and WE sure as HELL make a difference to and for the World in which WE all live!

When people, like YOU, like me, like WE, make a resolution (especially on New Year's Eve), WE do sure in the hopes of, with the thoughts of, with the intent of change, and by so changing that which WE believed needed to be changed, a desired outcome would be attained.

Well, all of US know, and only too well from years of experience and / or testamonials, that many of OUR attempts at these resolutions take on a LIFE of their own, and while being worked upon, a NEW World emerges before OUR eyes, captivating US as if WE are seeing OUR World with the eyes of a child, a World with infinite possibility and promise!

At such moments, its as if our mind and our heart have met and become friends with OUR Soul, bathed in the brilliance and the glory of that which CAN BE if only we would continue to forge ahead, to do that which MUST be done to achieve success!

Sometimes during OUR attempts at these resolutions, WE lose OUR sight, run into obstacles never imagined, question OUR ability or willingness to sacrifice that which need be, are filled with self doubt, lose our FAITH in ourselves, in others.

Well, I'm here to tell YOU straight out; Resolutions are good! Why? Because for whatever the reason, the cause of YOU making that resolution made it necessary for YOU to; at some point STOP, think, and decide that LIFE could NOT go on the way it was, CHANGE was necessary, and necessary NOW!

"Come what may", the consequences f any decision, CHANGE was necessary! Well I'm no rocket scientist, but if change was needed so quickly, and so strongly that YOU finally made a decision (making the resolution), and then YOU acted upon it, any progress in that direction benefited YOU, and by so doing, the World in which WE all live as well.

If YOU have read anything that I have written, YOU know how strongly I believe in having FAITH and BELIEF in GOD, and how often I tell YOU straight out that WE are not alone nor will WE ever be, there are Angels amongst US. I kid YOU not!!!

I'm not going to bore you or scare you into believing that which simply IS; I'm just going to say flat out; "What have YOU got to lose if YOU are so at the point in YOUR life when YOU made a decision to make a resolution (to change something), HAVE FAITH AND BELIEF IN GOD ABOVE, AND ASK HIM, ASK HIM FOR HELP to make it so?

YOU HAVE NOTHING TO LOSE, and EVERYTHING to gain!

You will be amazed, brilliantly amazed at what happens next, things happen (yes much because of YOUR effort, but "coincidences" appear to happen, only they are NOT coincidences), things and people that help progress or perhaps steer YOU in a better and more timely direction!

With the birth of each and every child, WE are all reminded in no uncertain manner, that GOD has not given up on MAN, that being the case, do YOU honestly think HE would abandon YOU if YOU asked for help? If YOU answered YES, WE both know YOU are lying! HE wouldn't, YOU just lost YOUR WAY.

And now, I'm just helping YOU find YOUR WAY back (coincidence? What do YOU think?).

Bottom-line; Children are held in OUR arms, HIS HOPE for MAN could NOT be more clear!

Look within YOUR mind and heart, encourage your family and friends to look within their minds and their hearts, find YOUR passion, pursue it relentlessly with FAITH, with BELIEF. YOUR resolutions, YOUR need to change, YOUR obstacles, YOUR "coincidences", were meant to help YOU, for help is all around YOU if only YOU BELIEVE, IF YOU HAVE FAITH, IF YOU ASK!

If it were not for my FAITH, my BELIEF inGOD above, I would not be here!

Just look into the eyes of OUR children and YOU will see, WE are not alone nor will WE ever be!

I believe in YOU, I believe in ME, I believe in WE, and WE CAN DO BETTER!

DARE TO BE YOU, I'LL DARE TO BE ME, and WE WILL DO BETTER! Shall WE begin?

52. "WHAT AMERICA MEANS TO ME"

What America means to me, HOPE!

With the birth of each child, GOD reminds all mankind that HE has NOT given up on us, that there is HOPE!

All around the globe, people of every shape and size, speaking a variety of languages, with differing traditions, cultures, some living amidst filth, rubble, chaos and despair surrounded by death and destruction, some living large in the lap of luxury, elegance, pomp and circumstance, many living as if time stood still, each day a seemingly endless duplicate of the day before; from somewhere, from someone, somehow, they hear of a place called AMERICA!

A place where "some of them have gone and not returned, not because of death, but because of LIFE, not because of pain and suffering, but because of joy and happiness of heart, not because of disease or amputated limb, but because of treatment / cure and the use of a limb. These people, the ones that have not attempted the journey yet, still in the place of their birth, have dreams too; of that which could be, of that which will be for themselves, their children, those they love, if only they can make it to "that place, AMERICA"!

They cross deserts, swim infested waters with predators literally tearing them to pieces, they fight attackers and win, die or temporarily surrender to prevent death and make a plan to try again, often subjected to unbelievable cruelty, abuse, brutality. Then they fight again! They sell their possessions, sometimes the clothes off their backs. They sell that which they have to offer, unbelievable sacrifices; their blood, their organs for safe passage for their children (often not knowing, that after they are dead, their organs removed, their children are sold into slavery).

But little do the captors realize that the children have a fire already burning within them, a fire burning with but one word, one name, AMERICA! And so, when the time is right, with all their might, THEY FIGHT; their captors, the elements, the circumstances, and move on (for nowhere do they have to return), there is but one direction, at whatever the cost, TO AMERICA!

The day comes, sometimes many years it took, sometimes hours, but it came, and before their eyes they see:

The Statue of Liberty, welcoming them, and although the words inscribed upon her base may be too distant for them to read, the words ring true within their hearts;

"GIVE ME YOUR TIRED, YOUR POOR,
YOUR HUDDLED MASSES YEARNING TO BREATHE FREE,
THE WRETCHED REFUSE OF YOURTEEMING SHORE,
SEND THESE, THE HOMELESS, TEMPEST-TOSSED TO ME,
I LIFT MY LAMP BESIDE THE GOLDEN DOOR!" Emma
Lazarus

One thing is certain, unless you are of American Indian ancestry, every single one of US or OUR ancestors, are or were, similar to them, from somewhere else, and came here to AMERICA for what it gave US / them, HOPE (for the dreams WE / they already had in mind, in heart). The HOPE was to fuel OUR / their FAITH, and to feed OUR /their SOUL!

What AMERICA means to me, HOPE! Like the birth of each child being GOD'S way of reminding US all HE has not given up on Mankind, that HE has HOPE, AMERICA fills me with HOPE that WE CAN DO BETTER!

For AMERICA is not one person, one dream, AMERICA is ALL of US, People of every shape and size, speaking a variety of languages plus one common one, English (allowing communication, commerce, LIFE to be more easily understood and shared, and defended if need be), with FREEDOM to have tradition, culture, religion, to pursue happiness knowing in all OUR hearts and minds that each and every one of US is significant, does make a difference, and that an attack against ANY one of US, is an attack on ALL of US, and JUSTICE will prevail equally!

WE, are people, and people by nature make mistakes for a variety of reasons and circumstance. That doesn't necessarily justify the mistake nor should it necessarily allow it to be tolerated.

That is why OUR Forefathers declared OUR independence, and accepted OUR Constitution as the LAWS for which, and of which, "WE the People of this united Nation" would abide, and defend. That is also why there has always been a means to amend that which has been written, and accepted as LAW, to allow US (the People of this Nation) to right something that time has proved wrong or that circumstances have shown US a need for updating.

That is precisely why to me, AMERICA means HOPE, for like the newborn child is a reminder that GOD HAS NOT GIVEN UP ON MANKIND, AMERICA, a Nation of "WE the People" (not some of US, all of US), reminds US OUR future is before US. The future is not yet written, it is before US, and like those that have come to OUR shores, there is no going back! There lies OUR greatest asset, "WE the People" ARE AMERICA, and WE will write OUR History by the choices WE make "this day", and in the days still to come! WE elect fellow citizens to represent US, WE approve and accept LAWS that serve and protect US. WE do not have to tolerate or accept anyone thinking or acting "above OUR LAW", because they are NOT> Because the future is not yet written, if WE need to change something, WE CAN, legally with OUR consent!

What AMERICA means to me, HOPE! That by OUR example, all OUR children will learn, grow, participate, gain confidence, discover their passion, pursue it relentlessly, share their blessings for all to see. That OUR children will have families of their own, futures of their choice, safety, and security. That OUR children once grown, will know their many blessings and assist others in their hours of need with a hand UP, not with a sustained hand-out.

What AMERICA means to me, HOPE! That by pursuing OUR dreams for better products and services, management, creativity, research and development, production will stimulate growth and advancement in all fields, jobs will be created, and OUR economy will be strong.

What AMERICA means to me, HOPE! That all of US will feel secure within OUR homes, OUR schools, OUR churches or places of worship, on OUR streets, in OUR towns, in OUR States, within OUR Borders. That when and if WE travel abroad, and become a victim of a crime or injustice, WE are defended, JUSTICE is served, and WE are brought HOME! That as WE go about OUR day, if WE see an injustice, witness a criminal act, WE help however WE can to stop it, and to prevent it from happening again!

What AMERICA means to me, HOPE! That WE will always be strong enough to defend OURSELVES, only send OUR Nation's Sons and Daughters into harm's way as a last resort, and once sent, support them with all OUR might, all OUR resources for a specific purpose, and when it is accomplished, they come HOME!

What America means to me, HOPE! That WE learn OUR History and not repeat that which failed, that WE balance harmony and beauty with necessity, and not waste or destroy that which is precious. That WE work with Nature, not against it. That WE realize, acknowledge in manner and action, that the LIFE of OUR Planet, like OUR lives, is finite, and GOD willing, will continue for hundreds and hundreds of years.

What AMERICA means to me, HOPE! That the realization; "That today is the tomorrow, of yesterday that has now passed", and by living THIS DAY to its fullest, by maximizing that which WE can accomplish today, by doing the best WE can, the promise of tomorrow is grander, and closer at hand!

What AMERICA means to me, HOPE! For YOU see, I BELIEVE IN YOU, I BELIEVE IN ME, I BELIEVE IN WE, and OUR future is not yet written! Shall WE begin?

53. HEALING HANDS, SO UNDENIABLY POWERFUL ARE TWO SIMPLE GESTURES

So undeniably powerful are two simple gestures that the majority of US are capable of offering with no expense to ourselves or others save for mere moments of OUR time and thought!

Have you every seen the reaction of a child who has just started to walk when a parent or loved one outstretches their arms with hands extended and palms facing the heavens? With shear delight and strength from within, the child practically launches himself / herself towards the loving arms awaiting his / her arrival. The excitement, and delight of the todddler reaching such arms and being rewarded with warm loving embrace, warms even the stiffest of hearts and brings a smile to ones face.

When a person addresses a crowd, be it small or large, and gestures in same manner, instantly are all present drawn within and made to feel as if included, a part of something grander, something of meaning, of significance, almost spiritual in nature are they called from within. And need not a word be spoken, the reaction is the same, but when coupled with heart-felt word of merit or purpose, the results can be staggering!

Be it with one or many, think back upon the times when such arms reached out to YOU, be it in joy or sorrow, how well received were YOU in such arms? Were YOU not strengthened or awakened to a power beyond one's self? Did not a wonderfully empowering strength seem to encourage YOU that YOU were not alone, and together YOU would face that which would come next?

With one simple gesture fright took flight, strength defeated exhaustion, and sunshine appeared on the dreariest rainy day. One simple gesture and a person, a People, a Nation or Nations felt not neglected, but included, considered, acknowledged! How powerful is that!!

To know ones heart, and to master the use of such simple a gesture, could not a World be made better? Would not such use of YOUR HANDS be HEALING HANDS?

When YOU are met with outstretched arm, hand openly extended, do YOU not feel welcome, even in a stranger's house? How simple a task is it to extend one's arm, un-clinch one's fist, and offer a hand to shake? Depending upon circumstance, climate, and / or culture, maybe simpler in one place than another, but worthy of the attempt. It too, has but an empowering effect upon all who bear witness. Fright turns to might, warmth and compassion brings understanding, and appearance of common ground from which progress can and will be made fills the air with that which can be, HOPE reigns!

Think of all the times YOU were met with outstretched hand beckoning YOUR touch, were YOU not relieved that conflict would most probably NOT follow, that friendship or at least tolerance of an opposing view would be heard? Could not compromise or negotiation be pursued from the start? How beneficial to be the one who puts such HAND out first, clearly leading by example!

How much wasted time and energy could be saved by so simple a gesture? Would not YOU benefit from displaying such example?

To know ones purpose, to hear that which is within one's heart, and to use this too, another so simple a gesture well timed, would not such outstretched Hand be a HEALING HAND?

Two simple gestures costing not a dime, a person answering the call from within their heart, significant one and all!

And if such hands, in so simple a gesture, are HEALING HANDS, is not GOD'S HAND at work as well?

DARE TO BE DIFFERENT, DARE TO BE TRUE, DARE TO BE
BOLD, DARE TO BE YOU! YOU are significant, as are WE all,
and OUR WORLD is all the better when WE are active in it! Shall
WE begin?

54. SO SIMPLE A TASK, HAVE NOT YOU PERFORMED?

I awoke from a dream so vivid, I thought I had not ben sleeping, although from my surroundings of darkened room and covered with bed linen it became apparent I must've been!

I dreamt of that which each of YOU (as well as I previously, months and months ago), have done countless times before, so simple a task that YOU will think me an idiot for even having to give it conscious thought; the task of simply putting on a pair of socks, and more specifically, the sock upon the right foot!

For YOU see, that simple task, requiring mere seconds for most (myself included months and months ago), "was" as of October 2012, a painful and difficult task, one that as each day passed became ever more painful, and ever more difficult to accomplish! So painful, and so difficult did it become, that I often hid my attempt from my family when so attempted!

As the months progressed, and pieces within me deteriorated, longer did it take in my attempts to do so simple a task, and I was found out by family.

By the time a surgery date for corrective action came, Sept 30, 2013, the pain of attempting that simple task was beyond belief and required near 10-15 minutes to accomplish each time.

And so, once surgery was completed, new pieces placed within me, and recovering was I, YOU can imagine how anxious was I to once again be as YOU, stand upon my own two feet, walk, and yes, put my socks on without pain, and in mere seconds without conscious thought!

But that did not happen, because recovery required caution, patience, and TIME for that which was now within me to heal correctly! So, only with the aid of an assisted device could I attempt and accomplish so simple a task. And at that, without pain being present, "I was thrilled, quite pleased with myself, and thankful to GOD"!

For near four weeks now, with the help of many a HEALING HAND, and four grueling hours of exercise per day, great progress has been made in mind and body! And then this dream did I have, as vivid as if I had done the task as YOU do daily, and I awoke!

So what did I do? NEED YOU ASK? YOU guessed correctly, I PUT MY RIGHT SOCK ON WITH MY OWN HANDS, AND IN MERE SECONDS!!!!!!!!!!!!!!!!!!!! Thrilled is not the word, for I KNOW GOD'S HAND WAS AT WORK ON MY BEHALF!

And that "my now so simple task" occurred this morning, SUNDAY (the Lord's Day), Oct 27th 2013, was indeed a wonderful reminder of how blessed I have been, and am this day!!!

Was not the HEALING HAND of GOD at work for YOU as well as for ME this day, for did YOU not feel the "JOY" in YOUR heart as well for accomplishing "so simple a task", one that required not a cent, just mere FAITH and BELIEF that it WOULD BE?

Have a wonderful day, and be ever so joyful in all that YOU do, for WE are all blessed!

DARE TO BE DIFFERENT, DARE TO BE TRUE, DARE TO BE BOLD, DARE TO BE YOU! WE are all significant, each and every one! WE all have HANDS that can HEAL if WE hear that which is within OUR heart and choose to listen! Shall WE begin?

55. SO GRAND A VIEW DID I
CHANCE TO SEE

Nearing home early Sunday morning while driving west, as so often I do when returning from the Bagel Shop, so grand a view did I chance to see; the leaves on the trees were bursting with vibrant color so wonderfully magnificent it near took my breath away! Even in the limited light and against a darkened partly cloudy western sky, the colors of newly turned Autumn leaves were so, so very magnificent!

And then, as if GOD had granted me a Good Morning gift, the light from the rising Sun behind me bathed the uppermost treetops as if in golden glow, and the vibrant colors exploded BEYOND BELIEF! As the Sun rose higher behind me, and the Sun's light traveled further down the trees towards the good Earth, the magnificence of Nature's Beauty, of Leaves of such color simply demanded that I stop the car, and praise GOD for having blessed my eyes so!!

Oh how I wished I had been a talented and gifted photographer (as so many of my Friends on Facebook are), and that I had a camera with me, for never did I want to share so beautiful a sight with all the World as that which was before my eyes, and forever now within my heart!

To think how might have missed such beauty be, for often have I traveled and did not see! Might not the same be for one and all?

With the miracle of LIFE granted through OUR parents by GOD, within US lies a passion and a purpose to someday be found when WE look within OUR mind and heart and hear that which calls, and then WE pursue it!

To write, to teach, to sing, to make music, to create, to act, to heal, to capture with paint or camera beauty as it be, to express, to discover, to explore, to challenge, to defend, to serve and protect, to risk, to dance, oh how fortunate and blessed WE be!

And when OUR passion be it found, and with OUR purpose WE go round, OURWORLD is discovered and truly found in every shape, sight, and sound!

So to each and everyone this I do ask and pray, as YOU go about YOUR day with YOUR PASSION AND YOUR PURPOSE BEING YOUR WAY, share YOUR gift from GOD above! For WE, and all OUR WORLD are all the better for it!

DARE TO BE DIFFERENT, DARE TO BE TRUE, DARE TO BE BOLD, DARE TO BE YOU! FOR "YOU" ARE SIGNIFICANT!

Shall WE begin?

56. A HEAVENLY MOMENT

When my wife Diane and I went to Disney World in September 2008 (the first and only four day vacation have WE taken together), one evening after dinner time, we found ourselves on Main Street in Magic Kingdom as the Sun was beginning to set.

After buying ice cream (she loves cones, I love cups), with ice cream in one of each of our hands, and while holding hands with the other, we strolled South on Main Street until we got to the Courtyard near the train station. There, we sat on a bench facing West. Once we sat, I started to eat my ice cream (Diane had been enjoying hers ever since we left the shop), and the Magic of The Kingdom truly sunk in, IT WAS WONDERFUL!

There we sat, enjoying ice cream, enjoying each others company, witnessing hundreds and hundreds of visitors experiencing The Magic of The Kingdom, hearing laughter, seeing golden smiles upon the faces of the little ones, all the while bathed in the brilliance of the golden glow of the setting Sun!

To me, it was a Heavenly Moment experienced while on Earth, for LIFE in the simplicity of THAT moment, could not have been any better, it was as I hope and pray Heaven to be (at least for US, when the time does call).

And so, to each and every one of YOU, do I hope and Pray, that YOU be firm in YOUR FAITH and BELIEF, that when one in YOUR FAMILY passes on, YOU can envision where they may be, and with whom by their side. For me, it's Main Street Magic Kingdom, sitting with the woman I love as we eat ice cream facing West as the Sun sets, bathed in the brilliance of GOD'S ALMIGHTY GLORY, hearing the sounds of childrens laughter, seeing couples in warm loving embrace, with not a care in the world except for capturing THAT moment!!

May YOUR vision be as grand for YOU, and those YOU love, if not, no worry; Take a trip to Disney and let them show YOU how its done! Have a magical day! Shall WE begin?

AUTHOR'S WISH FOR YOU

May YOU look within your mind and your heart, find your passion, your purpose, and pursue it relentlessly as best you can. May YOU "know of" many things through your experiences, and "KNOW" the power of; FAITH, of BELIEF, of LOVE, and that "NEVER, NEVER DO WE WALK ALONE".

And until then, until "YOU KNOW", always will Icontinue to write of FAITH, of BELIEF, of GOD.

DARE TO BE DIFFERENT, DARE TO BE TRUE, DARE TO BE BOLD, DARE TO BE YOU! For YOU are significant! And OUR WORLD is all the better for "YOU" having to be in it!

Semper Fidelis (Always Faithful)!

Daniel G. O'Leary

P.S.—I believe in YOU, I believe in ME, I believe in "WE"! Shall WE begin?